TALKINENDER

A GUIDE TO NONSEXIST COMMUNICATION

TALKING GENDER

A GUIDE TO NONSEXIST COMMUNICATION

RUTH KING

WITH CONTRIBUTIONS BY

MONIQUE ADRIAEN

DANIELLE BEAUSOLEIL

C M DONALD

SUSAN EHRLICH

TERRY LAVENDER

SHERRY ROWLEY

VALERIE VANSTONE

Copp Clark Pitman Ltd.
A Longman Company
Toronto

ISBN: 0-7730-5123-6

Editor: Barbara Tessman
Cover & interior design: Steve MacEachern
Typesetting: Carol Magee
Printing and binding: John Deyell Company
Permission to reprint photographs, illustrations, and layouts was granted by: Agence Science-Presse; Domal Marine Industries; Jacques Goldstyn; Interface magazine; Reuters News Agency; Andrew Stawicki; Toronto Star Newspapers Ltd.; York University Department of Communications

Canadian Cataloguing in Publication Data

King, Ruth Elizabeth, 1954–
Talking gender

Includes bibliographical references.
ISBN 0-7730-5123-6

1. Sexism in language. 2. Nonsexist language. 3. English language – Usage. 4. English language – Sex differences. 5. French language – Usage. 6. French language – Sex differences. I. Title.

P120.S48K56 1991   306.4'4'082   C91-093627-7
c.2   L8075

Copp Clark Pitman Ltd.
2775 Matheson Blvd. East
Mississauga, Ontario
L4W 4P7

Associated companies:
Longman Group Ltd., London
Longman Inc., New York
Longman Cheshire Pty., Melbourne
Longman Paul Pty., Auckland

Printed and bound in Canada by John Deyell Company

1   2   3   4   5   5123-6   95   94   93   92   91

C O N T E N T S

Chapter 4 Unequal Word Pairs
Danielle Beausoleil and Ruth King 22

Chapter 5 Job Titles
Monique Adriaen and Ruth King 27

Chapter 6 Feminizing French Discourse *Monique Adriaen and Ruth King* 41

Chapter 7 Terms of Address and Reference *Susan Ehrlich* 46

Chapter 8 Nonsexist Visual Images *Terry Lavender and Valerie Vanstone* 55

Chapter 9 Implementing Reform: Social and Political Considerations
Susan Ehrlich and Ruth King   71

Appendix A English terms   81

Appendix B French terms   85

Reference list   89

P

R

E

F

A

C

E

This guide to nonsexist communication grew out of the work of the York University Status of Women Communications Committee, which was founded by Ruth King, Advisor to the University on the Status of Women, 1989–91. York University has had a nonsexist language policy since 1985, and the university style guide (1986)♦ contains a short section on nonsexist usage. Unfortunately, passing a policy and providing a guide failed to eliminate nonsexist usage on campus. We still came across course titles featuring the so-called generic *man* and were regularly assailed by the sexism in the visual images found in campus publications. Clearly there was more work to do.

The communications committee was struck to explore avenues of education, to support those working (often in less than supportive atmospheres) against sexist language, and to deal with resistance to communication reform. We began by writing and producing a small pamphlet♦♦ explaining why the nonsexist language guidelines should be followed. Demand was instantaneous. We received requests for the guide from places as far afield as the Prairies and the Atlantic provinces, and the pamphlet is now in its third printing.

However, the pamphlet alone was clearly not sufficient. Nor were existing published guides to nonsexist language. Few of these guides present the rationale for language reform and, of these, the majority deal only with written language,

---

♦ The guide is now out of print, but the text (reproduced in the Status of Women periodical, *The Second Decade* 3, 2 (Dec. 1988)) is available from the Office of the Advisor to the University on the Status of Women, 309 Founders College, York University, 4700 Keele Street, North York, Ontario M3J 1P3; telephone (416) 736-5380.

♦♦ Ruth King and C M Donald, *Nonsexist Language,* 1990, 11 pages (available from the Status of Women Office, York University at $2.00 per copy).

ignoring verbal and visual communication. Readers needed more background information to understand the principles behind language reform. And, while there are pamphlets and short monographs addressing the problem of sexist language in French, no book we know of pays equal attention to the practical issues of creating nonsexist French discourse and job titles.

Our book is aimed at a general audience and can be used in a number of ways. Each chapter deals with a specific issue, providing the background and rationale for change and concluding with specific recommendations for nonsexist communication. Each chapter also includes suggestions for further reading. There are two appendices. The English appendix contains sexist terms (in alphabetical order) along with nonsexist alternatives. The French appendix gives masculine terms and their feminine equivalents (also in alphabetical order).

In nonsexist communication, we need to make a careful distinction between gender-neutral and nonsexist language. In most cases gender-neutral language does provide a nonsexist alternative, but sometimes gender-neutral language can confuse or obscure. For example, *marital violence* is a gender-neutral term that obscures the fact that almost all this violence is perpetrated by men and against women. Similarly, references to *parenting* tend to obscure the fact that most childraising is done by mothers.

Generic plurals, too, may give the appearance of gender neutrality while leaving male-centred content unchanged. Consider the following statement: "Many immigrants come to Canada each year. Their wives then have little access to language training." The generic plural in the first sentence, which should include all immigrants—male, female, married, unmarried, accompanied, and unaccompanied—is contradicted by the second sentence. The phrase "immigrants and their wives" implies that all immigrants are married men who bring with them some subsidiary attachments, or that married women are somehow less immigrants than are their husbands.

Many changes are required for women to achieve equality and visibility in society. Communication is a major area where change is needed, and in this book we focus on language reform. Yet it is important to note that sexist ideas dressed in nonsexist language remain sexist. For example, using "the worker...he or she..." and "the resident...he or she..." may, in some cases, be an adequate linguistic solution, but unless women's needs are discussed in the documents concerned, those documents remain sexist. A photograph showing equal numbers of women and men is still sexist if all the men are in positions of authority while the women are subordinate, or all the men active and the women sitting quietly. Classroom practice remains problematic if it incorporates the use of nonsexist language but still excludes women from the course content.

In writing this book, we have been aided by our common assumptions as feminists and university employees, but have attempted, in other ways, to reflect the diversity in our backgrounds. And, though we fully recognize that prejudice is expressed in language in the areas of race, class, religion, and mental and physical disability, to name but a few, we have confined our main attention to the issue of gender bias. Universities are largely white communities, and the authors of this book reflect this constituency; we do, however, differ in age, class, background, status, gender, and sexual orientation.

The writing of this book has truly been a co-operative effort. Chapters were written by those named as their authors, but the organization of the book and the content of the specific chapters were decided in group, and each chapter was extensively reviewed by all of us. C M Donald participated in the group meetings and edited the manuscript.

We wish to thank the following people for their comments, stories, suggestions, and support: Geneviève Adriaen, Hillary Allen, Peter Avery, Naomi Black, Anne Bokma, Deborah Esch, Gloria Georganas, Jila Ghomeshi, Josef Heim, Beth Hopkins, Phil Jackson, Suzanne Levesque, Donna Lillian, David Mendelsohn, Barry Miller, Raymond Mougeon, Margaret Reeves, Ann Roberts, Ian Smith, Johanna Stuckey, Marie-Josée Vignola, Bill Whitlaw, the staff of Founders College (York University), and Barbara Tessman, our editor at Copp Clark Pitman.

The Necessity for Reform

Ruth King

1

This book is about changing language and visual images to include women and their experiences. Language change involves both altering old usage to eliminate negative stereotyping of women and women's roles and creating new words to describe women's experiences.

Our aim is to present the reasons for reform, guidelines for nonsexist usage, and advice on implementing change. We will present guidelines for nonsexist writing and speaking both for English and French. We will also consider communication in a broader sense: we will present guidelines for producing and selecting nonsexist visual images.

LANGUAGE AND DIFFERENCE; LANGUAGE AND POWER

There are many gender-linked linguistic differences. They can be divided into two categories: differences in language use and differences in language structure. In the area of language use, Dale Spender (1985, 207) describes her research on mixed-sex conversations:

> In the hundreds of mixed-sex conversations I have taped there are virtually no instances in which the females—at least to begin with—do not accept the male perogative to legislate on language.... Women are "queried," they are interrupted, their opinions are discounted and their contributions devalued in virtually all of the mixed-sex conversations I have taped.

A large body of research beginning in the early 1970s provides evidence that women and men do indeed use language differently. As sociologist Pamela Fishman (1983) puts it, women do most of the conversational work; inequality is both brought to and constructed in male–female interaction. Research shows that women ask more questions, express interest in men's topics, and are generally "good listeners."

The social roles played by women and men are also reflected in language structure. Existing unequal power relations are reflected and reinforced in the use of such terms as *girl* and *little lady* to refer to an adult woman. This is equally true in the cases of other disadvantaged groups: *niggers* for black people, *queers* for lesbians and gay men, *loonies* for those diagnosed as mentally ill. Women are rendered totally invisible by allegedly generic terms such as *he* and *man* (as in "*Man* has made great strides in *his* pursuit of knowledge").

Why do these gender-linked linguistic differences exist? The literature on language and gender yields two main schools of thought. The first, which linguist Jennifer Coates (1986) calls the "difference approach," reasons that women and men belong to different subcultures and learn different ways of communicating. When male–female conversation breaks down, it is often because the participants are playing by different rules. For example, women often use questions to carry the conversation forward, whereas men see questions as requests for information. The woman may simply want to discuss a particular issue, but the man may feel obliged to provide definitive solutions.

This difference model also illuminates the ways in which women and men are represented in words. Because men have traditionally been the political leaders, the most acclaimed writers and artists, the grammarians, and dictionary makers, it is their worldview that is encoded in language. Many women writers have reported that the words and meanings they find in dictionaries constitute a foreign language for them. Women have written of the need to find a language to describe their experiences. Indeed, in her science fiction novel, *Native Tongue* (1984), linguist Suzette Haden Elgin creates a woman's language, Laadan, which more adequately expresses women's ideas.

Coates refers to the second approach to language and gender as the "dominance approach": men's dominance and women's subordination mean a hierarchical relationship between the sexes, and this situation is reflected both in language structure and in language use.

While some research tends to keep these two approaches separate, they are both clearly based on the notion of men's and women's unequal access to power. The dominance approach makes this explicit, using social inequality to explain why one sex does most of the conversational work and is negatively stereotyped or rendered invisible. The difference approach emphasizes the positive characteristics of women's linguistic "difference" despite the negative evaluations women's linguistic behaviour receives in a male-dominated society.

SEXISM IN LANGUAGE AND IN VISUAL IMAGES

The criteria developed by Mary Sykes (1985, 83) to help define linguistic discrimination against racial or ethnic groups can be used to decide when linguistic discrimination against women is present. We can assume an act of linguistic discrimination against women has occurred if:

1. there is a difference in the way men and women are treated;
2. this differing treatment is less favourable to women; and
3. the basis for the difference is gender related.

In our culture, for example, most of the terms we use to characterize women as sexual human beings are negative and demeaning; the opposite is true of terms for men. Consider the negative connotations of *slut* and the positive connotations of *stud*. Or consider the non-equivalent word pairs *spinster/bachelor* and *maître/maîtresse*.

As for sexism in visual images, magazine, billboard, and television ads are replete with visual images that show women as inferior or submissive and / or that show women and men in stereotypical roles.

We can classify types of sexism as follows:

1. male-as-norm (women invisible)
2. irrelevant reference to gender
3. irrelevant reference to physical appearance or domestic relationships
4. inappropriate forms of address
5. women ignored or objectified in visual images.

Male-as-norm (women invisible)

Each candidate should include three copies of *his* résumé with the application.

We'll be hiring the best *man* for the job.

In chapters 2 and 3, we will show that, for most people, the supposedly generic terms *man*, *l'homme*, and the pronouns *he/his/him/himself* are sex specific. We advocate replacing male terms such as *chairman* by true generics such as *chair*, and we offer guidelines for nonsexist pronominal usage. For French we suggest female equivalents of male terms, such as *chirugien/chirugienne*. Chapter 3 will deal with nonsexist solutions to the pronoun dilemma in English, and chapter 6 will look at the agreement system of French.

Irrelevant reference to gender

That *woman* dentist is really excellent.

In chapter 5, we will consider how to refer to people and the work they do. We advise against compound terms, such as *woman dentist*, and against terms with weakening suffixes, such as *sculptress*. For English we advocate gender-neutral terms, such as *chair*, and the reclaiming of former male-only terms, such as *sculptor*, to apply to both sexes. For French, given that it has grammatical as well as natural gender, we advocate male and female equivalents such as *agriculteur/agricultrice*, *avocat/avocate*, *auteur/auteure*, and *agent de change/agente de change*.

Irrelevant reference to physical appearance or domestic relationships

Susan Dixon, *a beautiful, green-eyed blonde*, has just entered her first year of medical school.

Penelope Wong, *wife of well-known lawyer James Wong*, will be working for a major downtown firm.

It is traditional for women's worth to be evaluated in terms of their physical appearance and domestic relationship. However, such references should be made (for both sexes) only where relevant to what is being described.

In chapter 7, we will discuss the use of *Ms*, *Miss*, and *Mrs.*, advocating the use of titles that indicate marital relationship only when it is known to be the preference of the particular woman.

Inappropriate forms of address

Hey honey! What's wrong? Don't you have a smile for me?

Could you get me a copy of that report, *dear*?

Chapter 7 will focus on appropriate terms of address in written and spoken communication among friends, co-workers, and strangers.

Women ignored or objectified in visual images

Women are often treated unequally in visual images. Advertisements, textbook illustrations, teaching materials, magazines, and newspaper photos either ignore women entirely or reduce them to objects. In chapter 8, we will discuss how to recognize sexism in visual images and how to find and use non-biased images.

OBJECTIONS TO REFORM

Language change—whether it is an attempt to avoid discrimination against women, people of colour, people with disabilities, or members of other minority groups—often meets with resistance. Here are some of the commonly heard objections to the use of gender-inclusive language, together with possible replies.

"But the dictionary says..."

People sometimes quote at length from the *Oxford English Dictionary* or some other work to prove, for example, that *man* refers to the species as a whole (or from *Le Robert* to prove the same for *l'homme*). Dictionaries reflect the usage of a particular period (or, in the case of etymological dictionaries, periods), and they reflect particular worldviews. They do not necessarily reflect the way in which language is used or interpreted today, nor its use by various social groups. Nor do they take into account the political and social impact of language.

As we shall see in chapters 2 and 3, numerous studies have shown that, regardless of traditional dictionaries, people of all ages, and women in particular, actually perceive *he* and *man* as gender-specific terms.

To see how different dictionaries reflect different worldviews, compare definitions in a recent *Webster's* to those given in Cheris Kramarae and Paula Treichler's *A Feminist Dictionary*. Take, for example, the word *housewife*.

Two role models: The woman above illustrates the most prevalent media image of women—a nameless escort for a male hero. Her body is decorative and functional, enhancing the man's prestige and displaying the logo of the male team. Although she has no connection to the story, editors at fifteen mass circulation newspapers chose to print this photo. The woman below is a respected scientist explaining new techniques in weather prediction. Her image ran in a university newsletter. It was not picked up by the major media.

> housewife—a married woman in charge of a household. (*Webster's Ninth New Collegiate Dictionary*, 1984)

> **housewife**—1. one of the acceptable roles for women;
> 2. unpaid additional employee for company who hires husband;
> 3. household worker who never reaches retirement age. (*A Feminist Dictionary*, 1985)

"But historically..."

Sometimes the etymology of the word is invoked to demonstrate its "real" meaning. "In Old English, *man* meant 'person.'" "*Homme* comes from the Latin and therefore it means 'human being.'"

If etymology is taken seriously, however, we might as well use *they* instead of *he* as the singular generic, a usage that stems from the mid-sixteenth century. In Britain, the use of *they* was so entrenched that it took an 1850 act of parliament to prescribe *he* as the accepted form (in standard usage) (Bodine 1975). The use of *chair* to mean presiding officer was first recorded in 1647 and thus predates the use of *chairman* by seven years. If etymological arguments are used to legislate specific usage, *all* the etymological facts should be considered.

One of the most telling arguments in the area of etymology is the fact that speaker–hearers are not linguistic historians; they are not aware of many facts about the history of their language. Human beings are born with an innate ability to acquire language and, on the basis of the data to which they are exposed (that is, the language they hear or see around them), they construct their own mental grammars without reference to the history of their language.

"It's too awkward..."

Those who regard *he or she* as clumsy ignore the frequency in English of co-ordinate structures such as *men and women, sooner or later*.

Others find the term *Ms* unpronounceable. This is mystifying since [mIz] rhymes with *his* [hIz], a word that gives English speakers no apparent difficulty.

Regardless of their perceived complexity (or lack thereof), all languages are readily acquired by native speakers. The perception of terms such as *he or she* or *Ms* as awkward must be regarded as a value judgment.

"You can't change language..."

Language changes. An example of change in meaning is that of the Modern English *hound*, which derives from the Old English *hund* (meaning "any kind of dog"). The meaning of *hound* has narrowed considerably over time. Conversely, the meaning of (Modern English) *dog* has widened; the Old English *docga* meant "mastiff."

Change is also evident when we compare our English to that of Shakespeare. In Shakespeare's writings, both main verbs and auxiliaries took *not* (as in "I deny it not") and main verbs came at the start of a question ("Revolt our subjects?"). In modern English, *not* only occurs with an auxiliary ("I do not deny it") and only auxiliaries are fronted to form questions ("Do our subjects revolt?") (Fromkin and Rodman 1983).

We can become aware of recent changes in a language by comparing the speech of younger and older generations. People in their sixties or seventies might still say "Is it they?" or "This is she," a usage highly unlikely to occur in the speech of a younger person.

Language change is a linguistic universal that can reflect changes in societal attitudes. The taboo words of one generation may well be acceptable to following generations. On the other hand, usage once considered as reflecting "the natural order" may well be rejected.

"This is trivial..."

Some argue that advocates of language reform should concentrate their efforts on "larger social issues." Language reform is essential, however, because language structure reflects the social roles that women, men, and all social groups play in society. For example, sexist language (such as the use of *girl* for *woman*) diminishes women's role in society. And though some suggest that societal change will produce changes in the language, it is apparent that the relationship between language and society works both ways: society affects language, and language, in turn, affects society.

In *Man Made Language*, Spender discusses the importance of naming women's experiences. For the social order to change, she points out, women must invest the language with their own meanings. To some extent we have been successful. Not long ago the word *sexism* did not exist, and the term *sexual harassment* was not commonly understood. Today the primary meanings of *chauvinism* (originally meaning "blind or excessive patriotism") and *sisterhood* are feminist-influenced ones.

"Nobody complains..."

There are various reasons why complaints may not be registered. Probably the most common is insecurity: students may well fear that a complaint would affect their final grades; office workers may hesitate to jeopardize their chances of advancement. Sometimes one simply becomes resigned to discriminatory usage or cannot face yet another battle.

The presence or absence of complaints should not be the deciding factor in changing gender-biased language. It should be changed because it is discriminatory and because it has a negative effect on girls and women.

FURTHER READING

John Berger, et al., eds., *Ways of Seeing* (London: Penguin, 1972).
♦ A general introduction to visual communication.

Matilda Butler and William Paisley, *Women and the Mass Media* (New York: Human Sciences Press, 1980).
♦ Provides a discussion of ways in which women and men are depicted unequally in print images.

Jennifer Coates, *Women, Men and Language* (New York: Longman, 1986).
♦ An overview of sociolinguistic research on language and gender, particularly in Britain.

Erving Goffman, *Gender Advertisements* (New York: Harper and Row, 1987).
♦ Categorises, with many illustrations, the kinds of images of women found in advertising.

Cheris Kramarae, *Women and Men Speaking* (Rowley, MA: Newbury House, 1981).
♦ A discussion of theoretical approaches to female and male use of language.

Dale Spender, *Man Made Language*, 2nd ed. (Boston: Routledge and Kegan Paul, 1985).
♦ A comprehensive analysis of how language, constructed by men, serves itself to construct male dominance over women. The main body of the second edition is unchanged from the 1980 first edition, but a preface has been added and the introduction revised.

Deborah Tannen, *You Just Don't Understand: Talk Between the Sexes* (New York: Morrow, 1990).
♦ About conversational misunderstanding between women and men.

Barrie Thorne, Cheris Kramarae, and Nancy Henley, eds., *Language, Gender and Society* (Rowley, MA: Newbury House, 1983).
♦ Provides an overview of language and gender research and includes an extensive annotated bibliography.

Mary Vetterling-Braggin, Frederick A. Elliston, and Jane English, eds., *Feminism and Philosophy* (Totawa, NJ: Littlefield, Adams, 1977).
♦ Contains a number of important articles on linguistic sexism.

Marina Yaguello, *Les mots et les femmes* (Paris: Petite bibliothèque payot, 1978).
♦ General discussion.

False Generics:

L'homme and Man

Ruth King

In this chapter, we will present the linguistic principles that form the basis of our analysis, as well as evidence that, whatever the traditional dictionaries say, *man* and *l'homme* are not generally considered generic terms. We will then present alternatives to sexist usage.

2

MAN WARS

In 1986, a lively debate was sparked by the Canadian government's search for a new name for its National Museum of Man/Musée national de l'homme. Communications Minister Marcel Masse set up a special committee to find a nonsexist name for the museum.

On the negative side, Senator Louis Robichaud decried the waste of taxpayers' money, declaring that *man* means "a member of the human species, and a woman [is] a man with a womb."♦ Author Pierre Berton, claiming to find himself "inadvertently" on the committee, denounced a "small, extreme minority of women," who would be better served if they were to "spend their time fighting for equal pay." He condemned the "silliness" of the enterprise, saying that it was "stupid and a gross misuse of the language to change words with 'man' in them."♦♦ Letters to the editor in a number of Canadian newspapers expressed equally strong views on the matter. The committee finally decided on the name: National Museum of Civilization/Musée national des civilisations (subsequently changed to the Canadian Museum of Civilization/Musée canadien des civilisations).

♦ "Non-sexist museum name ridiculed," *Toronto Star,* 8 Feb. 1986.
♦♦ "Berton writes of 'silly' name game," *Toronto Star,* 8 March 1986.

Such linguistic battles are fairly common, though not usually on a federal scale. Various municipal councils have debated the replacement of terms such as *alderman* with *councillor*, *manhole* with *access hole*, or *manhole cover* with *sewer cover*. In the university environment, replacement of *chairman* by *chair* has sparked letters of protest from faculty concerned about "the purity of the language" and "the integrity of words." Recommendations to change the titles of courses such as "*Man* and *His* Environment" are often met with appeals to academic freedom and photocopies of dictionary entries for *man*.

MORPHEMES: INDIVIDUAL UNITS OF MEANING

When we say that *man* is sexist, we are referring not to a sequence of letters *m-a-n* nor to a sequence of sounds pronounced [mæn], but to {man} the morpheme. Linguists define morphemes as the individual units of meaning that make up words. Not every syllable is a morpheme. The word *river*, for example, though composed of two syllables, contains only one meaningful element. *Chairman*, on the other hand, contains two syllables and two separate meaningful elements: {chair}, related to the verb *to chair*, and {man}, meaning "adult human male." *Human* contains two syllables but cannot be segmented into two morphemes because the sequence *hu-* is not an individual unit of meaning; *human*, referring to the species as a whole, consists of one morpheme.

Opponents of language reform often ridicule the feminist position on male terms such as *chairman* and *fireman* by maintaining that we also find objectionable words such as *manuscript* and *mandate*. A 1988 writer to the editor of the Kingston *Whig-Standard* referred to the "woman-mandate of speaking out against the ravages of sexist language." Tongue in cheek, he or she goes on to liken the cause to the importance of "The Battle Hymn-Hyrr of the Republic." However, the word *mandate* is not problematic, since it does not contain the morpheme {man}. In modern English, *mandate* is not segmentable into two morphemes (it comes from the Latin verb *mandāre*, "to command or commit," which in turn is compounded of *manus* "hand" and *dāre* "to give"). Similarly, *manuscript* comes from *manus*, "hand," and *scrībēre*, "to write."

The morpheme {him} is problematic only when used to refer to the species as a whole. We are not concerned with its homophone *hymn*, which has a very different meaning. For gender-inclusive language, words such as *freshman*, *craftsman*, *grantsmanship*, *groundsman*, *layman*, and *man-made* certainly are problematic. Unrelated words and morphemes that may happen to be spelt alike or sound alike pose no problem.

In French, we focus on {homme}, the morpheme meaning "adult human male," not on any sequence of identical sounds or letters. *Ver*, "worm," *vers*, "verse," and *vert*, "green," for example, are separate morphemes, though pronounced identically. Words like *homonym*, "a word which sounds the same as another but has a different meaning," are based on the Greek *homos*, "same," not on the Latin *homo*, and thus do not contain the morpheme {homme}.

Homo is, in any case, the generic Latin word for *man* (as opposed to animals); *vir* is the Latin for *man* (as distinct from woman). Confusion nonetheless ensued, since the ancient Romans were as prone to sexism as are contemporary North Americans. This is the confusion that has led to lesbians insisting on the phrase *lesbians and gay men* rather than the generic term *homosexuals* (of mixed origin,

Greek *homos* and Latin *sexus*), since this now tends to be understood as meaning men only.

WHAT DOES *MAN* MEAN?

Those resisting language reform often say that the meaning of *man* is clear: context alone allows us to distinguish between its sex-specific and its generic use. However, since the early 1970s, researchers have studied what children, high school students, and adults understand when they encounter the term *man*. Studies summarized by Wendy Martyna (1978) show that, in response to the generic *man* and *he*, women, men, and children alike form mental pictures of males, thus seriously undermining the efficiency of *man* and *he* as generic terms. Further, we encounter intended sex-specific usage far more often than generic usage. (Martyna's research yields estimates ranging from four to ten times as often.)

Researchers have also found that use of sexist language has markedly negative effects on women. John Briere and Cheryl Lanktree (1983) found that women rated a career in psychology as more or less attractive in direct proportion to the use of nonsexist or sexist language in the career description. When gender-exclusive language was used, women were less interested in the career. Signe Dayhoff's 1983 study of evaluations of women running for political office found that the use of sexist language in campaign literature resulted in female candidates being more negatively stereotyped. Mary Crawford and Linda English (1984) found that women students recall information more efficiently when gender-inclusive terms such as *people, his/her*, and *he/she* are used.

A 1973 study by Sandra Bem and Darryl Bem directly demonstrates the negative consequences of job advertisements containing *he/man* language. The researchers composed three versions of a job advertisement. In all three cases, the duties listed were identical, but varied terms were used to refer to the position. The first advertisement used *linesman* and the pronoun *he*. The second used *linesperson* and *he or she*, while the third used *linesperson* and only the pronoun *she*. More women applied in response to the inclusive language of the second advertisement (*person, he or she*) than to the exclusive first one (*man, he*). Notably, more still applied in response to the specific language of the third advertisement (*person, she*).

NONSEXIST ALTERNATIVES IN ENGLISH

The false generic *man* can be avoided in a number of ways:

1. Instead of *man, men,* and *mankind*, use *person/people, human being(s),* and *humanity.*

   Man must learn how to care for the environment.
   ➤ *People/human beings* must learn how to care for the environment.

2. Instead of *no man*, use *no one.*

   To boldly go where *no man* has gone before.(from the "Star Trek" TV series, circa 1960s)
   ➤ To boldly go where *no one* has gone before. (from the "Star Trek: The Next Generation" TV series, circa late 1980s)

One's *fellow man* can become simply *people, citizens, friends,* or *human beings*:

Concern for one's *fellow man* should be instilled from an early age.
➤ Concern for other *people* should be instilled from an early age.

3. Occupational titles can be altered to remove {man}:

freshman ➤	first-year student
garbageman	garbage collector
groundsman	groundskeeper
fireman	firefighter
barman	bartender
cameraman	camera operator
craftsman	craftsperson
mailman	letter carrier

4. The following commonly used terms containing the morpheme {man} can be easily replaced:

man-made ➤	manufactured, synthetic
manpower	staff, human resources
grantsmanship	grant-getting ability
workmanship	craftwork, work, artisanship

NONSEXIST ALTERNATIVES IN FRENCH

Generic usages of *l'homme* and *les hommes* can be replaced in the following ways.

1. Instead of *les hommes,* use *les êtres humains, les hommes et les femmes,* or *les gens.*

l'inégalité parmi *les hommes*
➤ l'inégalité parmi *les êtres humains*
➤ l'inégalité parmi *les hommes et les femmes*

2. Instead of *l'homme,* use *la personne.*

les droits de *l'homme*
➤ les droits de *la personne*

3. Sometimes the sentence can be recast to employ an indefinite pronoun such as *quiconque* or both feminine and masculine forms such as *tous et toutes* and *ceux ou celles.*

Ceux qui s'intérèssent . . .
➤ *Ceux et celles* qui s'intérèssent . . .

4. Feminine equivalents of male job titles can be formed.

homme d'affaires   ➤   *femme* d'affaires

Alternatively, male and female alternatives without *homme* can be used.

homme politique ➤ politicien
                          politicienne

Truly gender-neutral solutions do not exist in French as they do in English, since French has grammatical gender (all nouns are marked either masculine or feminine) as well as natural gender.

SPEAKING AND WRITING: DEALING WITH SEXIST QUOTES

People are often more successful at using nonsexist language in writing than in speaking, simply because writing is a more deliberate act (one usually has time to think and find the correct word). During heated discussion, old expressions such as "we've got to find the best man for the job" may slip out, or an initial "he or she" may be subsequently replaced by "he." However, acquiring nonsexist usage is like acquiring a first or other language. One improves with practice.

In both speaking and writing we face the problem of quoting material containing sexist language. In some cases, we can choose to quote another source. For example, in the 1973–74 York University undergraduate calendar, the department of sociology and anthropology used this quotation from the writings of Emile Durkheim to introduce their program information:

> As a condition of their acceptance into the sociological fraternity, we ask *men* to discard the concepts they are accustomed to apply to an order of facts, in order to re-examine the latter in a new way. (p. 234)

The practice of beginning a department's entry with a quotation has since been abandonned. However, it would surely be possible to find a relevant quotation that did not include sexist language. Likewise we can avoid quoting proverbs such as "A *man's* home is his castle" and "A *man* is known by the company *he* keeps." Either rework the proverb using nonsexist language (e.g., "*Our* home is *our* castle," "A *person* is known by the company *he or she* keeps") or use a nonsexist proverb (e.g., "There's no place like home," "Birds of a feather flock together").

We do not, of course, recommend that particular writers not be studied simply because their work contains sexist language. That would drastically reduce most fields of study. We do recommend that, wherever possible, you avoid the use of sexist quotations. When, for whatever reason, you wish to retain a quote with sexist language, there are several ways to indicate that the wording is problematic. In speaking, signal your awareness of the problem through the use of "quote/un-quote" or by introducing the material with phrases such as "what is referred to as" or "as the author says."

In a written quotation, [*sic*] can be used:

> C'est dans et par le langage que *l'homme* [*sic*] se constitue comme sujet. (Benveniste 1966, 259)

However, several instances of [*sic*] can be distracting, as in the following example.

> [The] idea—that a *man's* [*sic*] language moulds *his* [*sic*] perception of reality, or that the world a *man* [*sic*] inhabits is a linguistic construct—although in one form or another a very old one, has become associated with the names

of the Americans Edward Sapir (1884–1939) and Benjamin Lee Whorf
(1897–1941), and more particularly with the latter. (Sampson 1980, 81;
emphasis added)

Where quotations contain many instances of the so-called generic *man* or *l'homme*,
attention can be drawn to these through a comment included in square brackets
at the end of the quotation (e.g., [we assume the writer intends *man* to refer to the
species as a whole]). Another possibility for writing is to use ellipses and square
bracket insertions, as in "[The] idea—that . . . [people's] use of language
moulds . . . [their] perception of reality . . . ."

FURTHER READING |

Dennis Baron, *Grammar and Gender* (New Haven: Yale University Press, 1986).
♦ Provides an historical account of word meanings and the attempts of grammarians to
impose "a natural order" on usage.

Canadian National, *Les uns et les unes: Guide de communication non sexiste.* Available in English
as *Striking a Balance: A Guide to Nonsexist Communication* (Montreal, 1988).
♦ A twenty-eight page pamphlet containing nonsexist communication guidelines.

Council of Ontario Universities, *Employment Equity for Women: A University Handbook*
(Toronto, 1988).
♦ Includes a section on nonsexist language and visual images.

Margrit Eichler, *Nonsexist Research Methods: A Practical Guide* (Boston: Allen and Unwin,
1988).
♦ There is a section containing guidelines for nonsexist language usage.

Fédération canadienne des enseignantes et des enseignants, *Le langage non-sexiste: guide de
rédaction* (Ottawa, 1985).
♦ The major focus is on job titles.

Francine Frank and Paula Treichler, *Language, Gender and Professional Writing* (New York:
Modern Language Association, 1989).
♦ Contains articles analysing sexism in language; guidelines for nonsexist writing.

Jeanne Lapointe and Margrit Eichler, *On the Treatment of the Sexes in Research/Le traitement
objectif des sexes dans la recherche* (Ottawa: Social Sciences and Humanities Research Council
of Canada, 1985).
♦ Provides guidelines for nonsexist usage.

Rosalie Maggio, *The Nonsexist Word Finder: A Dictionary of Gender-Free Usage* (Boston: Beacon
Press, 1988).
♦ Contains alternatives, explanations, or definitions for over 5000 words and phrases.

Ministère de l'Education du Québec, *Pour un genre à part entière: guide pour la rédaction de
textes non-sexistes* (Quebec, 1988).
♦ Contains suggestions for feminizing French discourse.

Office de la langue française du Québec, *Titres et fonctions au féminin: essai d'orientation de
l'usage* (Quebec, 1986).
♦ The focus here is job titles.

Barrie Thorne, Cheris Kramarae, and Nancy Henley, eds., *Language, Gender and Society* (Rowley, MA: Newbury House, 1983).
♦ Contains articles by Donald Mackay and Wendy Martyna on the *he/man* debate.

Mary Vetterling-Braggin, Frederick A. Elliston, and Jane English, eds., *Feminism and Philosophy* (Totawa, NJ: Littlefield, Adams, 1977).
♦ Containing Janice Moulton's important article "The Myth of the Neutral Man."

A number of professional organizations for academics, including the American Philosophical Association and the American Psychological Association, have published their own guidelines.

A number of computer programs aimed at eliminating sexist language are available, including MacProof for Macintosh computers and Grammatik for IBM machines. These programs search the text for sexist and racist expressions. (The reader should beware, however, of the thesaurus options provided by word processing programs since they may well be sexist and racist in the choices they offer for synonyms.)

C H A P T E R

Pronouns in English

Ruth King and Sherry Rowley

3

WHAT *HE* MEANS ▌

Although many women feel excluded by the generic use of *he*, both men and women who champion this usage insist that the speaker's intentions are more important than the hearer's interpretation. As we saw in chapter 2, though, the use of terms like *man* and *he* has been found to have serious negative effects: they are not commonly understood to refer to both women and men.

The use of false generics actually reinforces sexist stereotypes. Consider the following example:

> The law student must work very hard to earn *his* degree.

The sentence most likely calls up the image of a male law student. Douglas Hofstadter (1986, 137) calls this a "default" image or assumption: the "simplest" or "most likely possible model" of the subject under discussion. Even though we know that a lawyer may be a man or a woman, our default assumption tends to be that the lawyer in question is a man, and the generic use of *he* reinforces this. Conversely, our default assumptions are challenged by statements like the following:

> A good secretary clears *his* desk at the end of the day.

PRONOUNS IN ENGLISH AND IN SOME OTHER LANGUAGES ▌

Sometimes we meet the claim that the traditional use of English pronouns is inherently correct and cannot be altered. Yet the provision of pronouns varies greatly from one language to another.

All languages have pronouns for the first (*I*), second (*you*), and third (*he, she, it, they*) persons. Yet there is a great deal of variation in what other information is conveyed by the pronouns. Standard English has only one second-person pronoun, *you*, whereas French has two, *tu* and *vous*. In English, gender is only indicated by the third-person singular pronouns (*he, she*). The third-person plural pronoun (*they*) is not gender-specific. Standard French distinguishes gender in both the third-persons singular (*il, elle*) and plural (*ils, elles*).

There are many other patterns. Tagalog, spoken in the Philippines, does not distinguish between masculine and feminine in the third person at all. Mandarin Chinese, on the other hand, marks masculine and feminine in its written form, but not in the spoken language. Indeed, even this distinction was introduced into written Chinese only after contact with speakers of western European languages.

Tegulu, a Dravidian language spoken in India, has four sets of third-person pronouns:

		Singular	Plural
Male	(very informal)	waadu	
	(informal)	atanu	waaLLu/waaru
	(formal)	aayana	
	(very polite)	waaru	
Female	(very informal)	adi	
	(neutral)	aame	waaLLu/waaru
	(formal)	aawiDa	
	(very polite)	waaru	
Non-human		adi	awi

Tegulu also has a parallel set of pronouns (*wiiDu, idi,* etc.) for people who are physically nearby. On the least formal level, there are only two subject pronouns (*waadu* for a male human and *adi* for anything and anyone else including a woman, a dog, and a shoe).

These examples show that the English pronominal system is far from being the only possible pattern. They suggest that no language is unalterable. Indeed, the pronominal systems of a given language may well change over time. English once commonly used the second-person singular forms *thou/thee/thine*, though these are now to be found only in particular dialects or in restricted (usually religious) contexts.

ALTERNATIVES TO *HE*

Use *he* only when the referent is clearly male. Use *she* when the referent is clearly female.

> After taking a women's studies course, a *man* may find that *he* now understands the situation faced by women every day.

> The mature *woman student* is frequently faced with a more restricted schedule than the younger student, because *she* often has the added responsibilities of children and domestic chores.

The so-called generic *he* can be avoided in a number of ways.

1. Replace *he* with *she or he* or *he or she*. Replace *himself* with *himself or herself, him* with *her or him*. In choosing between nonsexist alternatives we recommend alternation or alphabetic precedence.

> A person should vote for the candidate who impresss *him*.
> ➤ A person should vote for the candidate who impresses *him or her*.

> It is the task of the *chairman* to do what *he* can to make sure the meeting runs smoothly.
> ➤ It is the task of the *chair* to do what *she or he* can to make sure the meeting runs smoothly.

2. In writing, replace *he* with *he/she, she/he*, or *s/he*.

> When encouraging a team a coach may feel *he* needs to address individual members' needs.
> ➤ When encouraging a team a coach may feel *s/he* needs to address individual members' needs.

S/he, though popular, is controversial. Francine Frank and Paula Treichler (1989, 161) object to its usage on the grounds that it has no possessive or accusative case equivalents and that it cannot be pronounced. Others object on aesthetic or linguistic grounds since the slash is not at a morpheme boundary. Similar objections could be made to *fe/male* and to *wo/man* (*s, fe,* and *wo* are not individual morphemes). However, advocates of *s/he* give aesthetic and political reasons for adopting it, and point out that it saves space in print.

3. Use *they* as an indefinite singular pronoun.

> Anyone may participate if *he* likes.
> ➤ Anyone may participate if *they* like.

As we noted in chapter 1, the use of *they* as a singular pronoun has a longer history than is generally thought. It was used, for example, by writers such as Jane Austen and Jonathan Swift.

Some maintain that it is confusing to use *they* as a singular pronoun because it could also mean more than one person. However, the second person, *you*, is subject to the same problem, and no major campaign has been mounted to change it.

Frank and Treichler (1989) warn that the singular *they* still tends to be frowned upon in professional writing. We use it in both speaking and writing but warn the reader that such usage may be less acceptable to prescriptivists than some of our other alternatives.

4. Replace the generic *he/him/his* with the generic *she/her/hers*.

> A writer should write about *his* own experiences.
> ➤ A writer should write about *her* own experiences.

This method is used by Deborah Cameron (1985). After explaining that she uses *she* and *her* as "sex-indefinite referents" in her book, she notes (p. vii):

If there are any men reading who feel uneasy about being excluded, or not addressed, they may care to consider that many women get this feeling within minutes of opening the vast majority of books, and to reflect on the effect it has.

On the grounds that the majority of union members are female, the York University local of the Canadian Union of Educational Workers/Syndicat canadien des travailleuses et travailleurs en éducation (CUEW/SCTTE) uses *she* as a generic both in its constitution and in its collective agreements with the university administration.

Both Cameron and CUEW/SCTTE seek to draw attention to the invisibility of women through the use of pronouns. However, the use of *she* as a generic, while undoubtedly good for political effect, is open to the charge of reverse discrimination and can be seen as repeating the mistakes of the past.

5. Rewrite the sentence in the plural.

> A novelist should write about what *he* has experienced.
> ➤ Novelists should write about what *they* have experienced.

> A social scientist should take care that *his* work is not androcentric.
> ➤ Social scientists should take care that *their* work is not androcentric.

6. Use the indefinite pronoun *one*.

> If a student has problems *he* can always take another course.
> ➤ *One* can always take another course if problems arise.

The use of *one* sounds rather formal in modern English, and is best used in formal style.

7. Restructure the sentence to eliminate the use of a pronoun.

> The student with a disability may feel more at ease if *he* explores the campus prior to *his* first day of classes.
> ➤ The student with a disability may feel more at ease through exploration of the campus prior to the first day of classes.

8. Where possible, overtly include yourself and others by using first- and second-person pronouns.

> The anthropologist should take care that *his* work is not androcentric.
> ➤ As an anthropologist, *I* take great care that *my* work is not androcentric.
> ➤ As anthropologists, *we* should take care that *our* work is not androcentric.
> ➤ As an anthropologist, *you* should take care that *your* work is not androcentric.

Sensitivity is needed in choosing when to include oneself. The experience of white people, for instance, is not universal. In discussing the particular experiences of native North Americans, for example, it is inappropriate for white people to use *we* and *our*.

Further considerations

Some advocate alternating *he* and *she* in a text. While this might sound reasonable, it has a greater potential for confusion than most other solutions. Even if a reader can follow the writer's intent, this solution makes it easier to perpetuate sexist stereotypes, as in the following example:

> The student is required to complete *his* enrolment one week prior to the first day of classes .... Should the student change *her* mind, *she* must officially withdraw from the course or a failing grade will appear on *her* report.

Occasionally, when parallel texts are produced, one is written with generic *he* and one with generic *she*. For example, at the (bilingual) University of Ottawa, the faculty's 1990–93 collective agreement uses the generic *he* in the French version (except when dealing with maternity leave) and the generic *she* in the English version (except when dealing with paternity leave). While it does acknowledge the problem of sexist language, this solution is still problematic for the unilingual reader.

A written disclaimer that one is using the generic *he* and that it should be understood as including both males and females is offensive to many. We do not recommend it.

PUTTING NONSEXIST ALTERNATIVES TO USE

We have now established a number of alternatives to the generic *he*. In this section we show how these solutions may be employed in a text.

The following passage is from a memo written by a professor seeking a student assistant. Version A uses the generic *he*. Version B is nonsexist, but only one strategy is used to eliminate sexist language: the resulting text is somewhat awkward. Version C, which employs several strategies, is both nonsexist and fluid.

Version A

> I am looking for a graduate student who would be interested in working with a fourth-year course in linguistics as a language informant. In particular, I am looking for a graduate student whose first language (the language *he* learned as an infant/child) must be native to India or Indonesia/Malaysia. The course is designed to give senior linguistics students the opportunity to analyse in considerable detail a language with which they are unfamiliar. The language informant plays a crucial role in the course; it is *his* language that is analysed, and *he* serves as the sole resource for students in the course. The students learn about the informant's language by directing questions to *him*.

Version B

> I am looking for a graduate student who would be interested in working with a fourth-year course in linguistics as a language informant. In particular, I am looking for a student whose first language (the language *he or she*

learned as an infant/child) is native to India or Indonesia/Malaysia. The course is designed to give senior linguistics students the opportunity to analyse in considerable detail a language with which they are unfamiliar. The language informant plays a crucial role in the course; it is *his or her* language that is analysed, and *he or she* serves as the sole resource for students in the course. The students learn about the informant's language by directing questions to *him or her*.

Version C

I am looking for a graduate student who would be interested in working with a fourth-year course in linguistics as a language informant. In particular, I am looking for a graduate student whose first language (*the language learned* as an infant/child) is native to India or Indonesia/Malaysia. The course is designed to give senior linguistics students the opportunity to analyse in considerable detail a language with which they are unfamiliar. The language informant plays a crucial role in the course; it is *the informant's* language that is analysed, and *he or she* serves as the sole resource for students in the course. The students learn about the language by directing questions to *the informant*.

FURTHER READING |

Many of the references given for chapter 2 are also applicable here.

Dennis Baron, *Grammar and Gender* (New Haven: Yale University Press, 1986).
♦ Provides a history of pronouns in English, including attempts—*tey, E, herm*—to find a new generic third-person singular.

Unequal Word Pairs

Danielle Beausoleil and Ruth King

4 In this chapter we will see that one linguistic aspect of women's subordination is demonstrated by the use of non-parallel descriptions. While words with positive connotations are applied to men's activities, the same or similar acts on the part of women are described with words carrying diminishing or negative implications.

WHY IS SHE SO BOSSY?

Many men we know are *informative, discursive,* or even *talkative.* They have been known to *register a complaint* or two. And they are certainly responsible about *reminding* others of their commitments. But why is it only women who are *gabby*? Does she really *bitch* all the time? And *nag*? Women *chatter*; men *discuss.* She is *aggressive, abrasive,* and *strident*; he *defends his position.*

These negative evaluations derive from sex-role stereotyping: the belief that certain activities are appropriate only to one sex or the other. Activities that elicit praise for women, draw criticism for men. And vice versa.

It is no coincidence that many of these examples involve women who play active roles. Helen Franzwa (1974) notes:

> As soon as females behave in ways that are viewed as being *strong* the offending behavior is labelled with a *strong* and, more importantly, a *negative* adjective. Instead of being confident, enterprising or energetic, she is called argumentative, crude and bossy—even worse!

LADIES AND GENTLEMEN █

Some of the most commonly discussed examples of linguistic sexism are word pairs such as *bachelor/spinster, lady/gentleman, governess/governor, mistress/master,* and *girl/boy.* The images of the carefree bachelor and the desiccated spinster make it clear that marriage is the only acceptable state for a woman, but that a man who escapes this trap is seeking the good life. (Innovations such as *bachelorette* simply have a diminishing effect, since they add a weakening suffix {-ette} to a male term.) *Governors* are rulers; *governesses* look after the children of others. *Masters* run the house; *mistresses* please the master. *Girls* have to wear dresses and keep clean, whereas *boys* run around the neighbourhood to play. When adult women are called *girls,* it detracts from their adult status and infantilizes them. Except when black men are called *boy* as an insult, men are only called *boys* in the context of being "one of the boys" or reaping the benefits of the "old-boys' network."

The term *lady,* while initially used to divide middle- and upper-class from working-class women, has since been used to prettify the low range of employment offered to women (i.e., *cleaning ladies;* note that the term *garbage gentlemen* is not yet in circulation). Indeed, the term *lady* seems now to have lost much of its association with manners, social class or, one might argue, politeness.

HISTORICALLY █

In "The Semantic Derogation of Women," Muriel Schulz (1975) traces the history of many of the derogatory words applied to women. Many of these words began with positive or neutral connotations but gradually took on negative connotations. For example, the word *hussy* (from Old English *huswif*), which originally meant the female head of a household, was later applied to a "rude or rustic woman," then to women in general, and finally came to mean "prostitute." *Girl,* originally a child of either sex, came to mean a female child. While the use of *girl* for a female child remains relatively intact, the word was then applied to adult women to denote first maidservants and then "the female sex—or that part of it given to unchastity." It is, as we note above, still a diminishing term when applied to adult women. Schulz points out that words for boys or men have not generally undergone this devaluation. This is understandable, since it is men who have defined the rules of grammar and the meanings of words.

SEXUAL TERMS █

Julia Penelope (then writing under the name Julia Stanley, in research reported in Eakins and Eakins 1978, 113) has analysed the sexual terms applied to women and men in English. She found some 220 for women and only 22 for men. This has to do not only with men's position as namers and definers but also with women's traditional status as sex objects. Male terms are aggressive and positive, such as *hunk, young buck;* female terms are passive and negative, such as *piece, pussy, cow.* A good example of a non-parallel word pair is provided by *slut/stud.*

There are those who vehemently object to the use of *gay* as a non-derogatory word for *homosexual,* complaining that this is stealing a word from "our" language. And yet the slang usage of terms such as *dog* and *chick* passes with no such objection.

IN FRENCH█

The patterns we have mentioned above are also apparent in French. Marina Yaguello (1978) notes that a man is *un brillant causeur* while a woman is *une bavasse* or *un moulin à paroles*. Men *contestent* but women *sont hystériques*.

In a survey similar to Stanley's, Yaguello checked the synonyms for *femme* given in various dictionaries and found that the number of negative terms far exceeded the positive terms and that the vast majority could be divided into two categories, *maman* and *putain*. In both cases, the woman is described in terms of physical appearance (*belle/moche*, *blonde/rousse*), and morals (*sainte/teigne* or even *poison*).

The same non-parallelism is found with word pairs. Consider the differences in meaning of adjectives when used with *homme* and when used with *femme*:◆

femme galante—"a loose woman"
homme galant—"a well-brought up man"

honnête femme—"a virtuous woman"
honnête homme—"a refined man"◆◆

This trend is also clear in the terms *un professionnel* and *une professionnelle*. The connotations of these words are identical to those raised in Robin Lakoff's (1975) famous example: "he's a professional" and "she's a professional." *He* is usually imagined to be a business executive, lawyer, or doctor, while *she* is often assumed to be a prostitute.

In the case of titles, there is a tradition in French of using feminine forms to refer to "the wife of." While *Monsieur l'ambassadeur* is unambiguous, *Madame l'ambassadrice* may very well be the wife of the ambassador rather than an ambassador who is a woman. This traditional usage is being challenged today, as we will see in chapter 5.

Non-parallel word pairs include *gouverneur/gouvernante* ("governor/housekeeper") and *couturier/couturière* ("fashion designer/seamstress"). Examples of semantic derogation along the lines found by Schulz for English also exist. Until the sixteenth century, *garce* was simply the female equivalent of *gars*, "guy." *Garce* then came to mean "prostitute," while *gars* has retained its neutral meaning. Originally *compère* and *commère* meant "godfather" and "godmother." Now *compère* means "friend," while *commère* means "a constant talker who bad-mouths others."

LETTERS OF RECOMMENDATION█

The praise that women and men receive may vary greatly. As we evaluate our hiring practices to ensure we are not discriminating against women and other disadvantaged groups, it is important to watch for differences in letters of recommendation.

Stereotyped language may well damn women with faint praise. Male candidates may be *brilliant thinkers*; female candidates may be *hard workers*. Nancy Jo

---

◆ Non-native speakers should consult unilingual French dictionaries such as *Robert* or the *Collins French–English Dictionary*. For example, the *Robert Méthodologique* (1987) gives under *honnête femme* "qui a une vie rangée, qui ne trompe pas son mari."
◆◆ These examples are taken from Yaguello (1978).

Hoffman (1972) found that, in letters for women candidates for academic posts, descriptions of physical appearance were not only included but were given the weight of "a thesis statement." Hoffman found, predictably, that referees included assessments of the relationship between women's family life and their ability to work at a full-time career. Referees also tended to discuss the qualities of the spouses of female candidates. Rather than discussing the academic qualities cited for male candidates, referees stressed the "feminine" qualities of female candidates: their co-operativeness, warmth, and rapport with students.

A more recent study by Carol Watson (1987) found inappropriate terms such as *pert, lovely, crisp, a joy,* and *irrepressible* used in letters written to support women candidates. As in the Hoffman study, referees discussed the physical appearance of female (but not male) candidates. And, equally stereotypically, more male candidates were said to have a sense of humour.

Spender (quoted in Watson 1987, 28) warns us to keep in mind, in our evaluation of letters written by men and women, that:

> women who write references rarely "gush"; many of their recommendations are models of relevant comment and dignified restraint, so "superb teacher," "researcher without peer," "academic of inordinate intellectual stature," not to mention "genius" are not the descriptions that find favor in the assessments provided by women.

NONSEXIST SOLUTIONS

Avoid words that indicate negative stereotypes of women's roles in society, such as *cackle, nag, squaw, spinster, hag.* Replace with neutral terms such as *laugh, remind, native woman, single woman, woman.*

For French, too, describe women neutrally: talk about both *un brillant orateur* and *une brillante oratrice.* If you use conjoined structures such as *ladies and gentlemen, boys and girls,* and *mesdames et messieurs,* alternate the order.

Avoid stereotyping male and female roles in such outdated expressions as *the fairer (weaker) sex/the stronger sex, le beau sexe (le sexe faible)/le sexe fort.* Talk about *women and men, les femmes et les hommes.*

Some feminists have adopted the strategy of investing pejorative words with their own positive (and sometimes older) meanings. For example, Mary Daly and Jane Caputi (1987, 114) redefine the word *crone:*

> Great Hag of History, long-lasting one; Survivor of the perpetual witchcraze of patriarchy, whose status is determined not merely by chronological age, but by Crone-logical considerations; one who has Survived early stages of the Otherworld Journey and who therefore has Dis-covered depths of Courage, Strength, and Wisdom in her Self. *Examples a:* Harriet Tubman, rescuer of slaves, psychically/physically fearless Foresister *b:* Ding Ling, twentieth-century feminist activist and author, Survivor of multiple political purges, one of China's best-known and most prolific female writers.

Reclaiming the language by asserting woman-centred meanings is one way of changing the language altogether. Some single women have formed social organizations for *spinsters*. You must take care, particularly in writing, to make sure that the positive connotations either are explicit or are clear because of the context.

FURTHER READING▌

Mary Daly, *Gyn/ecology: The Metaethics of Radical Feminism* (Toronto: Fitzhenry & Whiteside, 1978).
♦ Contains discussion of "man made language" and the importance of investing sexist language with new meanings.

Mary Daly and Jane Caputi, *Websters' First New Intergalactic Wickedary of the English Language* (Boston: Beacon Press, 1987).
♦ Reclaims the language through creating new words and through investing old words with new meanings.

Cheris Kramarae and Paula Treichler, *A Feminist Dictionary* (Boston: Pandora Press, 1985).
♦ Documents women-centred meanings and analyses the history of words from a feminist perspective.

Robin Lakoff, *Language and Woman's Place* (New York: Harper and Row, 1975).
♦ This monograph is the best-known early work on language and gender. It inspired many others to do research in the area. Although today Lakoff sounds overly cautious about our ability to change the language, her discussion of how women are both stereotyped and silenced remains an important one.

Muriel Schulz, "The Semantic Derogation of Women" in *Language and Sex: Difference and Dominance*, ed. Barrie Thorne and Nancy Henley (Rowley, MA: Newbury House, 1975).
♦ Shows how terms designating women have taken on negative connotations over time.

Marina Yaguello, *Les mots et les femmes* (Paris: Petit bibliothèque payot, 1978).
♦ A general work that draws on early writings on sexism in language structure and that gives many French examples.

Marina Yaguello, *Le sexe des mots* (Paris: Belfond, 1989).
♦ A glossary of French words examining gender from a grammatical and sociohistorical perspective.

Job Titles

Monique Adriaen and Ruth King

In this chapter, we will review the linguistic mechanisms underlying existing masculine and feminine job titles. In order to create
nonsexist job titles we must use different strategies for English and
French. For English we advocate job titles that make no reference
to gender. For French we advocate separate male and female terms
because gender is an inherent feature of the French grammatical
system. English terms such as *actor/actress* and *salesman/saleswoman* can be replaced
by *actor* and *sales clerk* respectively. In French, however, we advocate the use of
female equivalents of male terms: *un biologiste/une biologiste, un avocat/une avocate*.
In the discussion of French strategies for creating new feminine forms, we will
compare usage in Quebec and France, noting stylistic differences.

NURSE–DOCTORS AND DOCTOR–NURSES

The title of this section comes from the experience of a friend who ran a medical
clinic in a rural, northern community a few years ago: she was the doctor and
worked with a male nurse. The townspeople found this "role reversal" rather
perplexing and, before long, began referring to the medical team as the "doctor-
nurse" (the female doctor) and the "nurse–doctor" (the male nurse), thus raising
the man's status and lowering the woman's.

In our society, women have only recently begun to enter the professions in
significant numbers, and they are still considerably underrepresented in most,
particularly in the areas of science and technology. Because women have lacked
financial and administrative control, and because they have lacked power as

critics, as academics deciding reading lists, and so on, women's art and writing have always been largely invisible in mainstream culture.

Not surprisingly, then, many occupations have had male-only titles: *businessman/homme d'affaires*. Female "equivalents," as we saw in chapter 4, are rarely that; for example, both the English *authoress* and the French *autoresse* have weak and/or derogatory connotations. Terms such as *woman lawyer* and *femme docteur* are demeaning because they imply that women in these professions are deviations from the norm.

JOB TITLES IN ENGLISH

Creating nonsexist job titles in English essentially involves providing alternatives for compounds with *man* and eliminating female terms with weakening suffixes. We also advocate against adding *woman* to a title (*woman executive, woman chiropractor*) to "let people know" that the professional is not a man. Refer simply to *executives, chiropractors, secretaries,* and *nurses*.

Replacing compounds with *man*

In chapter 2, we mentioned some terms for which nonsexist alternatives already exist, such as *fireman* ➤ *firefighter, policeman* ➤ *police officer*. The English appendix contains our suggestions for replacing a number of such compounds.

In choosing nonsexist alternatives, we tend to avoid (where possible) using *person*, as in *fireperson, policeperson*, even though these are linguistically plausible solutions. Unfortunately, the use of *person* has moved from being neutral through being coy (*waiter* ➤ *waitperson*) to being a euphemistic term for women (*chairwoman* ➤ *chairperson*). This last is exacerbated when the terms are used as a pair (e.g., *chairman* used for males; *chairperson* for females).

Replacing terms with weakening suffixes

In the arts, there are a number of word pairs in which the terms designating men take the suffix *-er/or* or no suffix at all, while the term designating women takes the suffix *-ess* as in:

singer ➤	songstress
author	authoress
sculptor	sculptress
poet	poetess
actor	actress

The members of these pairs differ in connotation. A *poetess* would not be seen as being as serious as a *poet*, and certainly not as talented. We note, too, that although the term *actress* is in common usage, a number of women now refer to themselves as *actors*. On the model of gender-neutral terms such as *writer, teacher,* and *speaker*, we advocate adding the morpheme *-er/or* to the stem of a verb to produce the relevant noun.

In more limited usage is the suffix *-ette* used to designate women, as in *majorette, jockette* (recorded by Eakins and Eakins (1978) as the female equivalent of *jockey*;

now used as the female equivalent of *jock*), (computer) *hackette*. The suffix *-ette* has also been used to refer to women in other contexts, such as the use of *bachelorette* (as diminishing as *spinster*). We recommend discarding the suffix *-ette*.

We replace *bachelor*, *spinster*, and *bachelorette* with the gender-neutral *single person*. On those few occasions when it is relevant that marital status and sex be specified, we advocate *single woman/single man*, *unmarried woman/unmarried man*. *Jocks* we leave as *jocks*, regardless of sex, and *hackers* as *hackers*.

JOB TITLES IN FRENCH

In French every noun is marked either feminine or masculine. Gender is a part of the language and not necessarily linked to biological sex: *la* fille; *le* garçon; *la* table; *le* pupitre. In these examples, the definite article (feminine *la*, masculine *le*) marks the gender of the word.

The use of grammatical gender has led searchers for nonsexist alternatives towards the recognition of, indeed the creation of, gender-marked feminine forms rather than the use of gender-neutral, traditionally masculine forms. This has been particularly the case in the area of job titles.

Feminizing words according to the rules of the language is one easy way to promote visibility and equality for women and to speak and write more accurately and precisely. As Hélène Dumais (1987, 3) points out, feminine terms are already well recognized for professions traditionally open to women, such as *infirmière*, *institutrice*, and *vendeuse*.

As more women enter professions once dominated by men, new terms must be created to designate their new roles. Many language users and dictionary makers, however, hesitate to form feminine equivalents for professions previously accessible only to men.

Attitudes toward language reform may differ, and the reasons for resisting it vary. It is generally acknowledged that, in the area of nonsexist language, Quebec has shown a more progressive and informed attitude than has France. France has a long tradition of purism and prescriptivism in language matters, carefully upheld by such institutions as the Académie française. Grammarians decree that the masculine shall be considered neutral or generic. Even well-known feminist thinkers (such as Elizabeth Badinter, Simone de Beauvoir, Luce Irigaray, and Marina Yaguello) are regularly referred to by such masculine terms as *auteur*, *écrivain*, *chercheur*, and *professeur*.

In addition, psychological and sociological factors come into play. Some feminizing suffixes such as *-esse* and *-ette* seem to have a pejorative or derogatory value. In many cases, lack of prestige and power is associated with the feminine form: one balks at *une contrôleuse des finances* (an administrative position) but not at *une contrôleuse d'autobus* (the ticket collector on a bus).

Sometimes ad hoc attempts at language reform have led to grammatical aberrations such as "madame la directeur," "elle est la première sous-directeur aux finances," "elle a été nommée recteur de l'Académie de Paris et chancelier des universités" where the article, the adjective, and the past participle all agree in gender with their referent (feminine) but not with the noun that they modify (masculine). Systematic change, however, is possible, as innovations such as *avocate, compositrice*, and *historienne* show. Traditional grammatical rules can readily be used to form new feminine equivalents as they are needed.

In what follows, we review the basic grammatical rules for the formation of feminine nouns. We then look at problem areas in the grammar where, for example, no feminine form presently exists. Lastly, we present guidelines to remedy these problems.

HOW TO FEMINIZE FRENCH NOUNS ▮

French grammar uses a number of different linguistic strategies to create feminine equivalents of masculine nouns.

Regular nouns ▮

1. The most common way of forming masculine/feminine pairs is to add -*e* to the masculine written form, and to pronounce the final consonant of the masculine oral form. (The masculine form is on the left; the feminine form is on the right.)

étudiant ➤ étudiante
avocat   avocate

2. In general, nouns ending in an oral (non-nasal) vowel do not change their pronunciation in the feminine. Certain dialects may lengthen the final vowel in the feminine form.

ami ➤ amie
abonné   abonnée

3. If a masculine noun ends in a nasal vowel, this nasal vowel becomes an oral vowel in the feminine, and the final nasal consonant is pronounced.

voisin ➤ voisine

4. The final consonant can be doubled and an *e* added.

criminel ➤ criminelle
champion   championne

5. In certain cases, the final vowel or consonant sound changes in the feminine form.

étranger ➤ étrangère
veuf   veuve

Suffixes ▮

A second way to form masculine/feminine pairs is to use masculine and feminine suffixes.

1. *-eur/euse* (note the change in the pronunciation of the vowel)

chanteur ➤ chanteuse
danseur   danseuse

Not all masculine job titles in -*eur*, however, have a feminine equivalent in -*euse*. In some cases, a feminine form does not exist in traditional French grammar. We will deal below with the feminization of words such as *chercheur* and *metteur en scène*.

2. -*teur*/*trice*; -*deur*/*drice*

auditeur	➤	auditrice
lecteur		lectrice
ambassadeur		ambassadrice

3. the addition of the suffix -*esse* to the masculine form

prince	➤	princesse
hôte		hôtesse

Although common in Old French, this suffix is less usual in contemporary French. Some forms in -*esse* are poetic, legal, slang, or archaic. Many have been replaced by a more contemporary form.

chasseur	➤	chasseresse (poetic)
demandeur		demanderesse (legal)
gonze		gonzesse (slang)
docteur		doctoresse (archaic)

Special cases

Certain words borrowed from other languages form their feminine by adding -*ine*.

tsar	➤	tsarine
speaker		speakerine

In popular speech, the feminine is formed by adding -*te* to the masculine form of certain words.

voyou	➤	voyoute
rigolo		rigolote

Epicene words

According to Maurice Grevisse (1988, 794, sec. 476.b) epicene words are words existing in only one form, either masculine or feminine, which refer to both sexes.

une girafe—"a male or female giraffe"

un hippopotame—"a male or female hippopotamus"

Epicene words referring to humans are usually masculine (especially in the area of professional titles), but this is not invariably the case.

un acrobate	un metteur en scène
un mannequin	un professeur
une vedette	une victime

Grevisse suggests that, to specify the sex, one needs to add *mâle* or *femelle* in the case of animals, *homme* or *femme* in the case of humans (e.g., *une souris mâle, une femme professeur*).

Other authorities, including the *Larousse Dictionnaire de Linguistique* and the Office de la langue française in Quebec, call words with two grammatical genders "epicene words." Such words usually end in *-e*.

un élève ➤ une élève
un astronaute   une astronaute
un chimiste   une chimiste

Problem areas █

The gender opposition can present difficulties when one member of the pair is missing. For example, traditional dictionaries give no masculine equivalent to *une sage-femme*◆ and no feminine equivalent to *un juge*. In French as in English, the masculine form is often taken to function as a neutral, generic form, and it is in most cases the feminine form that is missing. Many words ending in *-eur* fall in this category:

annonceur	défenseur
chroniqueur	professeur

as well as epicene words such as

acrobate	biologiste
anthropologue	diplomate

In some cases, the regular feminine form cannot be used as a feminine equivalent because it already exists in the language with a different meaning.

médecin—"the doctor"   médecine—"the field of medicine"
marin—"the sailor"   marine—"the navy"

Derivational difficulties may also result in the absence of a form. Sometimes it is not clear what the feminine equivalent of a masculine noun might be.

témoin ➤ témoigne?
témoine?
témoin?

In other cases, the regular feminine form is possible but is rarely or never used.

amateur ➤ amatrice
auteur   autrice
sénateur   sénatrice

◆ In an interview with Denise Bombardier, in the June 1983 francophone edition of *Châtelaine*, entitled "Denise Bombardier rencontre Benoît Groult" (p. 42), Groult mentions that the masculine term for *sage-femme* is now *maïeuticien*.

In still other cases, several feminine forms are possible, but there is no consensus as to which is the most desirable.

sculpteur ➤	sculpteur
	sculpteure
	sculpteuse
	sculptrice
chef	chef
	cheffe
	chève
	cheffesse

Another difficulty is the use of the suffix -esse which, as noted above, tends to have a pejorative, diminishing connotation.

poète ➤	poétesse
docteur	doctoresse

In the case of *maire/mairesse, ministre/ministresse* we run as well into the problem of the existing feminine form referring to "the wife of . . . ," as we saw in chapter 4. This is also traditionally the case for military titles.

général ➤	générale
caporal	caporale

However, this usage is gradually disappearing from the language, leaving the feminine forms free to take on new meanings parallel to the masculine forms.

Another difficulty is the difference in meaning between the masculine and the feminine forms. Consider the differences between *maître/maîtresse* and *couturier/couturière*.

One last difficulty deals with the case of homonyms, where the feminine form usually refers to the object, the machine, or the action.

un trompette—"a male trumpet player"
une trompette—1. "a female trumpet player"
           2. "a trumpet"

un balayeur—"a male sweeper"
une balayeuse—1. "a female sweeper"
          2. "a machine used for sweeping"

un manoeuvre—"a male labourer"
une manoeuvre—1. "a female labourer"
          2. "a manoeuvre"

PRINCIPLES AND GUIDELINES FOR FEMINIZATION

For the last fifteen years, Quebec linguists, dictionary makers, and translators have been studying the problem of sexism in French. Books, articles, and pamphlets dealing with the issue have appeared. Those from the Office de la langue française du Québec and various provincial and federal ministries are notable.

In 1986, the Office de la langue française published *Titres et fonctions au féminin: essai d'orientation de l'usage* in which it proposed five criteria for accepting new feminine forms (p. 7). To be accepted, a form must be:

1. regular: its formation must follow normal grammatical rules (e.g., *er/ère; -eur/euse; -teur/trice*, etc.);
2. analogical: there must be other nouns with the same endings (*banquier/banquière* is similar to *ouvrier/ouvrière*);
3. marked: there must be a distinct feminine ending in writing and speaking (*chercheur/chercheuse; écrivain/écrivaine*);
4. attested: the form must already occur in at least one dictionary or lexicon;
5. in use: a form that is not found in a dictionary may still be used to varying degrees (*autrice* is the regular feminine for *auteur*, found in dictionaries, but *auteure* is much more widely used).

The guidelines below follow these principles. In creating new feminine equivalents, we make use of the traditional rules of the language outlined above. Where there are several forms presently in use, we present them all and, where possible, advocate the use of one in particular. Our aim is to make masculine/feminine pairs as systematic and regular as possible.

E p i c e n e   W o r d s ▐

C l a s s   I   (w o r d s   e n d i n g   i n   - e)

Words ending in *-e* are easily feminized by using the feminine form of the articles: *une* or *la*. Do not use the masculine form to refer to a woman. Do not add *femme* to a masculine term. For example, when referring to a woman who is a dentist, do not say *un dentiste* or *une femme dentiste*; say *une dentiste*.
Similarly:

une capitaine	une notaire
une membre	une pilote
une ministre	une poète

Many of these words are still considered strictly masculine in France. For example, there are no feminine forms in the 1985 edition of the *Grand Robert* for *capitaine, membre,* or *notaire*.
Some words ending in *-e* already have a feminine in *-esse*:

maire	➤	mairesse
ministre		ministresse
notaire		notairesse

Traditionally, these feminine forms referred to "the wife of . . . ." As this meaning dwindles, the feminine forms are free to take on new meanings equivalent to the masculine. Thus, the Office de la langue française recommends the use of *mairesse* and *contremaîtresse* as the feminine of *maire* and *contremaître* respectively.

There is, however, also a tendency to use the epicene term with a feminine article and let the *-esse* form disappear (especially since many people see the *-esse* suffix as pejorative). Thus the regular form *poétesse* is increasingly being replaced with *une poète*. (Other forms, used especially in France, are *un poète* or *une femme poète*.)

For the sake of simplicity, we recommend the use of the feminine article with most epicene words ending in -e. The -esse feminine form should be used only when it is clearly established and accepted form. The word *maître* deserves special mention. In certain of its uses, the feminine is *maîtresse (maîtresse (d'un animal), maîtresse de ballet, maîtresse d'école, maîtresse de maison)*. We do not recommend changing these forms. In the other uses of *maître*, we advocate using the feminine article to feminize the masculine form (e.g., the French university titles *maître-assistante, maître de conférences, maître de recherches*, etc). The term of address for a female lawyer is *Maître*.

Certain words such as *une critique, une manoeuvre*, already exist but have another meaning. We agree with the Office de la langue française du Québec that identical pronunciations, especially in these cases, do not cause hopeless confusion: context and syntax can make the meaning clear.

C l a s s   I I

The second class of epicene words consists of those words, usually masculine, that refer to both sexes. To feminize these terms, simply use the feminine articles. Do not add the word *femme*: do not use *une femme médicin*, use *une médecin*. Similarly, the Office de la langue française du Québec recommends:

une chef	une matelot
une conseil	une substitut
une mannequin	une témoin
une marin	

Some possible feminine forms of *un chef (une chève, une cheffe, une chèfe)* are too unusual or too rare. The word *cheffesse* (sometimes *chéfesse*) does exist but is to be avoided because of its negative overtones. (It is interesting to note that the *Grand Robert* (1985) does not recognise a feminine form for *chef* but does in the case of *sous-chef* where it suggests *une sous-chef*.) Finally, *cheftaine* refers only to someone in charge of girl scouts.

The forms *une matelote* and *une substitute*, although possible, are extremely rare. The Office de la langue française du Québec therefore recommends the use of the epicene form.

The word *mannequin*, usually referring to someone of the female sex, is nonetheless masculine in gender. Its regular feminine form would be *mannequine*, but as the pair -in/ine is quite rare in French, the epicene form *une mannequin* is recommended.

W o r d s   e n d i n g   i n   - e u r ▮

C l a s s   I

Provided the noun form is derived from a verb, the regular feminine ending for nouns ending in -eur is -euse. For example:

acheter	un acheteur	une acheteuse

Although controversial, -euse has several advantages. First, it is already well-established in the language, so new feminine nouns in *-euse* will more readily be accepted. Secondly, it has the advantage of being marked both in the written and the oral forms: the masculine and the feminine forms differ in pronunciation and spelling. Thus to form the feminine of words ending in *-eur*, use *-euse*:

une camionneuse	une chercheuse
une chauffeuse	une programmeuse

Exceptions—e.g., *professeur/professeure*—are discussed below.

Some of these nouns *(chauffeuse)* are already to be found in the dictionary with other meanings, but context and syntax should be used to determine the intended meaning. Others, like *chercheuse*, already exist as feminine adjectives, which should make the use of new feminine noun forms more readily acceptable.

Although recommended here, the following forms are considered rare or marginal by the *Grand Robert* (1985): *arrangeuse, chauffeuse, débardeuse, détacheuse, mesureuse, outilleuse, recruteuse, soigneuse, tailleuse,* and *trempeuse.*

In some cases, particularly in Canada, there has been some reluctance to create new feminine forms in *-euse* for masculine nouns in *-eur*. Historically, the *-euse* ending was considered lower class. In modern usage, however, *-euse* seems to have lost most of its negative connotations and is being used more and more. We warn the reader, though, that the issue is still a controversial one for some.

Class II

A very small class of French nouns ending in *-eur* form their feminine in *-eure*.

un prieur	➤	une prieure
un supérieur		une supérieure

If users have negative associations with the *-euse* form in certain cases, the *-eure* ending can be used instead:

une annonceure	une professeure
une gouverneure	une superviseure
une metteure en scène	

The *-eure* feminine ending is used much more in Quebec than in France. The *Grand Robert* recognizes only one such form, *ingénieure. Annonceur, auteur, docteur,* and *gouverneur* appear only as masculine forms. It suggests a possible, although rarely used, form in *-euse* for *metteur en scène.*

The word *professeur,* derived from the Latin noun *professor* and not the French verb *professer,* has given rise to several feminine forms. The *Grand Robert* gives *professeuse, professoresse, professeur-femme,* and *professeur* as possible forms for the feminine. For reasons outlined above, we do not advocate the use of *professoresse, professeur-femme,* or *professeur.* Although the *-eur/-euse* opposition in French is very common, we reject *professeuse* for etymological reasons (i.e., *-eur/-euse* is reserved for nouns derived from verbs). We are thus left with *professeure* as a possible feminine form for *professeur.* This form has already gained wide acceptance in Quebec.

Words ending in -*teur*

The large class of words ending in -*teur* forms a feminine in -*trice*. Feminine equivalents are easily derived:

une conservatrice   une instructrice

Three words ending in -*teur* deserve special mention. They are *auteur, docteur,* and *sculpteur*. Several possible feminine forms have been suggested in various grammars and dictionaries for each. For example:

auteur ➤	autrice
	autoresse
	authoresse
	auteur
sculpteur	sculpteuse
	sculptrice
	sculpteur
docteur	doctoresse
	doctrice
	docteuse
	docteur

The form recommended here, and by the Office de la langue française du Québec, is the form in -*teure: une auteure, une docteure,* and *une sculpteure*.

At present there seems to be a difference in usage between *conservateur* and *conservatrice*. The feminine form is common in spoken, informal usage whereas the masculine term is more often used to refer to women in writing and in formal speech. We recommend the use of the feminine form for all cases.

Words ending in -*(i)er*

Words ending in -*(i)er* also constitute a very large class. They regularly form their feminine in -*(i)ère*. For example:

écolier ➤	écolière
conférencier	conférencière
boulanger	boulangère

Those words in -*(i)er* that have no recognized feminine form usually refer to those jobs and professions that have been restricted primarily to men. There are no linguistic obstacles to the creation of the proper feminine terms:

une bouchère   une menuisière
une banquière   une policière
une conseillère   une pompière
une financière

Some of these words already exist but with a meaning not strictly equivalent to that of the masculine form. *Bouchère*, for example, refers to the wife of a butcher or to someone who works in a butcher's shop rather than to a woman who slaughters animals for food. *Conseillère* is considered acceptable in expressions such as *conseillère matrimoniale* and *conseillère municipale*, but for administrative or political positions with more prestige the masculine form is still the most used, as in *conseiller d'Etat* (see Yaguello 1989, 56–57). (The use of *conseillère* seems more widespread in France than in Canada.) A similar prestige-based difference is evident in the pair *couturier* (fashion designer) and *couturière* (seamstress or dressmaker). However, as more women enter these professions, this difference should gradually disappear.

Certain words in *-ière* are considered marginal by the *Grand Robert*—e.g., *armurière, charpentière, menuisière, serrurière,* and *tôlière*. However, we recommend their use.

Nouns ending in *-t*, *-d*, *-n*, *-l*, and in a vowel

Nouns in these categories, if they do not already have a feminine form, can be feminized by adding an *-e* (and, in certain cases, doubling the final consonant).

une consultante une experte	une présidente
une doyenne une écrivaine	une électricienne
une consule une chargée de ...	une professionnelle une députée

Some of these forms (*doyenne, professionnelle*) already exist, but not as strict equivalents of the masculine terms. As the older meanings drop out of usage and as women gain access to these positions, the forms above will begin to function as true equivalents.

The word *conseil* is not feminized. The Office de la langue française du Québec recommends that it be considered as an epicene form. For example, *Titres et fonctions au féminin* (1986, 14) has:

un conseil juridique	➤	*une* conseil juridique
un économiste-conseil		*une* économiste-conseil

The *Grand Robert* accepts the feminine *chargée* in the expression *chargée de cours* but notes that in the case of *chargé de mission* the feminine is not used. We recommend the systematic use of *chargée* when a feminine form is needed.

Compound words

For compound words, each part can be feminized according to the rules outlined above.

une annonceure-présentatrice une briqueteuse-maçonne	une commis-vendeuse une lieutenante-gouverneure

A FRENCH SUMMARY █

1. Address yourself to everyone: avoid the masculine/generic terms.
2. Promote equal opportunity and equal visibility by using feminine equivalents whenever possible.
3. Avoid using compounds with *femme (une femme médecin)*.
4. To feminize:
   - use a feminine term that already exists in the language: *une savante, une contractuelle*
   - in creating new forms, follow the morphological rules of the language: *une productrice, une charpentière*
   - with epicene words, use the feminine articles *une* and *la*: *une chef, la membre, une témoin*
   - avoid the use of unusual neologisms or new terms: use *une chef*, rather than *une chève* or *une cheffe*.

FURTHER READING █

Else Boel, "Le genre des noms désignant les professions et les situations féminines en français moderne," *Revue Romane* 11, 1 (1976): 16–73.
♦ An empirical study of feminine forms for job titles in the French (France) press and media in the 1970s.

Hélène Dumais, *La Féminisation des titres et du discours au Québec: une bibliographie* (Groupe de recherche multidisciplinaire féministe, Université Laval, 1987).
♦ An important bibliography of works in French up to December 1986.

Rosalie Maggio, *The Nonsexist Word Finder: A Dictionary of Gender-Free Usage* (Boston: Beacon Press, 1988).
♦ Contains alternatives, explanations, or definitions for over 5000 English words and phrases.

Ministère de l'Education du Québec, *Pour un genre à part entière: Guide pour la rédaction de textes non-sexistes* (Quebec, 1988).
♦ Includes a clear and succinct section on the feminization of job titles.

Office de la langue française du Québec, *Titres et fonctions au féminin: essai d'orientation de l'usage* (Quebec, 1986).
♦ Written after wide consultation with grammarians, dictionary makers, and language users in France, Quebec, and other French-speaking regions, this comprehensive study of the feminization of job titles in French offers a range of alternatives and explains the reasons for their varying degrees of acceptance.

Marie-Josée Vignola, "Quelques applications de la féminisation des titres en classe de français langue seconde," *Revue canadienne des langues vivantes* 46, 2 (1990): 354–64.
♦ A discussion of putting nonsexist solutions into practice in the French-as-a-second-language classroom.

Marie-Josée Vignola, "Utilisation de titres professionnels masculins afin de désigner une femme: norme et usage," *York University Working Papers in Second-language Teaching* 2 (1987): 55–82.
♦ An empirical study of feminine forms for job titles in the French (Quebec) press and media.

Marina Yaguello, *Les Mots et les femmes* (Paris: Petit bibliothèque payot, 1978).
♦ One chapter deals specifically with the grammatical aspects of masculine/feminine pairs.

Marina Yaguello, *Le Sexe des mots* (Paris: Belfond, 1989).
♦ Both Yaguello's books deal mainly with French as spoken in France.

Feminizing French Discourse

Monique Adriaen and Ruth King

GENDER AND AGREEMENT IN FRENCH

6

We saw in chapter 5 that nonsexist linguistic strategies for French are substantially different from those for English because gender is an inherent feature of the French linguistic system. Because French, unlike English, has an elaborate system for ensuring that nouns, adjectives, and verbs are adjusted to agree with each other, different solutions are also necessary when we look beyond the level of choice of words. In this chapter we will address the problems for nonsexist writing and speaking presented by agreement between nouns and adjectives, nouns and past participles, and nouns and pronouns.

In French, adjectives and past participles agree in gender and number with the nouns they modify:

la petite fille	le petit garçon
les petites filles	les petits garçons
la fille est venue	le garçon est venu
les filles sont venues	les garçons sont venus

In traditional grammar, when an adjective or a past participle modifies both a masculine and a feminine noun, the adjective or past participle must be put into the masculine plural:

La fille et le garçon sont petits.
La fille et le garçon sont venus.

Similarly, the masculine plural pronoun *ils* is used when referring to a group of women and men, regardless of their actual numbers. If, for example, there are 120 women and one man in a class, then the masculine plural form of the noun, *étudiants*, and the masculine plural pronoun, *ils*, are used to refer to them as a group.

In French as in English, there is a long tradition of reluctance to allow change in the language. Language reform at discourse level has been even slower than reform in the area of job titles. However, for the reasons we have discussed in previous chapters, there is every reason to avoid the use of masculine terms as generic. Below we give a number of guidelines for "feminizing" written and spoken French.

ALTERNATIVES TO MASCULINE FORMS

1. Use the full feminine and masculine forms together.

> Il y aura des séances d'orientation pour les *étudiants* de première année.

> ➤ Il y aura des séances d'orientation pour les *étudiantes* et les *étudiants* de première année.

2. In writing, a popular alternative is to use parentheses, slashes, or hyphens.

> Cette conférence a été organisée dans le but d'aider les *plan-nificateur(rice)s* et les *enseignant(e)s* à intégrer l'égalité des sexes et des races dans le programme d'études des écoles primaires et secondaires.

> Les *consultant-e-s* sont priés d'envoyer leur rapport avant la fin du mois.

> Le congrès de la Société canadienne des *Pharmaciens/iennes* aura lieu au printemps prochain.

However, using slashes, parentheses, or hyphens is controversial. In *Pour un genre à part entière* (1988, 6–7) it is argued that these usages do not promote the visibility of women but rather treat them as an afterthought. Along with practical and political considerations, keep in mind that this usage is not aesthetically pleasing when used repeatedly in a long text. However, those in favour point out that using parentheses or hyphens is a spacesaver. (In *Pour un genre à part entière* changing font size is advised.) Others prefer the slash and full masculine and feminine words because they give the feminine form equal space with the masculine.

> Ce journal est connu pour la qualité du travail de ses *rédacteurs/rédactrices*.

3. Nouns that have only one form for both sexes can be pluralized.

> le chef ou la chef   ➤   les chefs

Use *le ou la* + noun and *un ou une* + noun sparingly. However, since some invariable nouns are traditionally associated with men, it is important to use a specific feminine form as much as possible simply in order to make clear that the word is being used generically.

les ministres ➤ le ou la ministre

4. To avoid stereotyping professional activities, an invariable form should be followed by both masculine and feminine pronouns, much as you would employ *he or she* in English.

Les actionnaires sont convoqués à une assemblée où *ils et elles* devront voter . . .

Les secrétaires ont le droit de poursuivre des cours de perfectionnement si *ils ou elles* le désirent.

In speech, we have heard *il . . . elle* (with a pause between the two pronouns), but most of the native speakers we have polled reject this usage as bizarre and favour *il ou elle*. As in English, the order of the pronouns may be reversed: *elle ou il*. There is some debate regarding the acceptability of *il et elle* and *ils et elles*.

5. Omit the article and adjective following the second of two nouns to make repetition less awkward.

les consommatrices averties et les consommateurs avertis
➤ les consommatrices et les consommateurs avertis

Since in this case, according to the rules of French grammar, the adjective is masculine plural, it is advisable to place the masculine noun closest to the adjective.

6. Similarly, when using *ils* or other pronouns to refer to masculine and feminine nouns, place the masculine noun closest to the pronoun.

Après que les *étudiantes* et les *étudiants* ont choisi leurs cours, *ils* doivent se procurer au plus vite leurs livres à la librairie.

Les *décoratrices* et les *décorateurs* doivent soumettre leurs projets avant le 31 mars s'*ils* désirent participer au concours.

7. Both the masculine and feminine forms of the following pronouns may be used together: *tous et toutes, chacun et chacune, ceux et celles, aucun et aucune, nul et nulle, pas un et pas une, certains et certaines,* and *quelques-uns et quelques-unes.*❖

Ceux et celles qui s'intéressent à la musique . . .

❖ In the singular, use *quelqu'un;* while *quelqu'une* exists, it is a rarely used literary term.

8. Try to replace those nouns that have the same pronunciation in the masculine and feminine with a true generic term:

> les élues et les élus
> ➤ les personnes élues
>
> les employées et les employés
> ➤ le personnel

9. In a long text, replace both masculine and feminine forms with collective nouns.

> les enseignants et les enseignantes
> ➤ le corps enseignant
> ➤ le personnel enseignant

Other collective nouns include *assemblée, collectif, collège, communauté, direction, effectif, ensemble de, gens, groupe, population, public, regroupement* (*Pour un genre à part entière* 1988, 13).

10. Sometimes the sentence may be rewritten.

> La personne choisie occupera un poste de *directeur*...
> ➤ La personne choisie occupera un poste à la *direction*...
> ➤ La personne choisie assumera la *direction*...
>
> On cherche des *candidats*...
> ➤ On sollicite *candidatures*...

11. In some texts, the first- and the second-person pronouns can be used to avoid the repetition of masculine and feminine forms, as was suggested in chapter 3 for avoiding the generic *he* in English.

> En tant que biologiste *il* a le droit de...
> ➤ En tant que biologistes *vous* avez le droit de...

USING NONSEXIST ALTERNATIVES ▌

Here are two versions of the same job advertisement. Version A is written according to the rules of traditional French grammar, while Version B is a nonsexist, smooth text.

V e r s i o n   A

Annonce d'un poste:

Traducteur

L'hôpital de West York est à la recherche d'*un candidat* pour un poste de *traducteur* dans son Service d'informations et renseignements. *Il* traduira en français la correspondence, les rapports medicaux et des documents techniques.

Le candidat choisi possédera un diplôme en traduction, des connaissances sur la terminologie médicale, et trois à cinq ans d'expérience en traduction.

Veuillez nous faire parvenir par écrit votre curriculum vitae avant le 1 mars.

Conformément aux exigences relatives à l'immigration au Canada, cette annonce s'adresse aux *citoyens canadiens* et aux *résidents permanents*.

V e r s i o n B

Annonce d'un poste:

Traducteur/Traductrice

L'hôpital de West York sollicite des *candidatures* pour un poste de *traducteur/traductrice* dans son Service d'informations et renseignements. *La personne choisie* traduira en français la correspondence, les rapports medicaux et des documents techniques.

Si *vous* possédez un diplôme en traduction, des connaissances sur la terminologie médicale, et trois à cinq ans d'expérience en traduction, nous vous invitons à nous faire parvenir par écrit votre curriculum vitae avant le 1 mars.

Conformément aux exigences relatives à l'immigration au Canada, cette annonce s'adresse aux *citoyen(ne)s canadien(ne)s* et aux *résident(e)s permanent(e)s*.

FURTHER READING **|**

The bulk of guidelines for French are devoted to job titles.

Ministère de l'Education du Québec, *Pour un genre à part entière: Guide pour la rédaction de textes non sexistes* (Quebec, 1988).

♦ This publication addresses the issues raised here and presents a comprehensive set of guidelines.

C H A P T E R

Terms of Address and Reference

Susan Ehrlich

In this chapter, we examine differences in the way that women and men are addressed and described, both in speaking and in writing. Women tend to be addressed or designated by terms that are more familiar than those used for men. The significance of this non-parallelism is discussed and alternative nonsexist terms are provided.

TERMS OF ADDRESS

Terms of address include the names, titles, terms of endearment, and so on that a speaker uses to establish or continue communication with the person s/he is talking to. Terms of address are forms used to say something *to* an individual or individuals, not *about* an individual (McConnell-Ginet 1978).

Research in sociolinguistics has shown that terms of address encode information about the existing social relationship between addresser and addressee. In particular, a difference in status between speakers will often be reflected by the use of asymmetrical or unequal terms of address.

In a classic study on the politics of address terms, Roger Brown and Albert Gilman (1960) demonstrate how the use of second-person pronouns in languages such as French, German, Spanish, and Italian is determined, to a large extent, by social factors. In French, for example, both *tu* and *vous* can have singular reference. When used to address a single individual, their assymetrical usage expresses a power differential between speaker and hearer: *tu* is used to address subordinates, *vous* is used to address superiors. On the other hand, the symmetrical use of *tu* expresses solidarity, and the symmetrical use of *vous* expresses social distance. In modern English (and many other languages) the *tu/vous* system is similar to the use of familiar and formal address terms.

Familiar terms of address, which are used among individuals of equal status to express solidarity, will also be used to signal the status difference between a superior and a subordinate. Likewise, more formal terms of address, which express social distance between people of equal status, can be used by a subordinate to express deference to a superior.

Consider the spoken forms of address used between individuals of differing status or power: boss/employee, professor/student, doctor/patient, adult/child. The subordinate individuals in these relationships will probably (at least initially) use a title in addressing the more powerful member of the pair (*Mr.* Rae, *Professor* Clivio, *Dr.* Klein). It is considered appropriate for the superior to use a familiar term (usually the first name) in addressing the less powerful member of the pair.

Empirical studies (Kramer 1975; Wolfson and Manes 1980) show that in service encounters female customers are more often addressed by familiar terms than are male customers. Men are most often called *sir*; women are regularly called *honey* and *dear* (by both men and women alike). This differing linguistic treatment of women and men can be seen as unfavourable to women: women receive the familiar terms of address associated with subordinate status, whereas men receive the more formal address reserved for those of superior status. Men in our culture will probably only receive terms of endearment from intimates. Women, on the other hand, receive terms of endearment from people they do not even know.

This type of familiarity from strangers can extend beyond the use of endearments. In North American culture, unacquainted persons in large urban centres will normally treat each other with silence. This convention is strikingly violated by men who whistle, stare, and direct comments at women who are strangers to them. Once again, women and men are treated differently, and women receive the familiarity reserved for low-status groups.

Deborah Tannen (1990a) points out that when talk-show hosts, panel moderators, and so on, address men and women with PhDs, the men are called by their academic title, *Doctor*, far more often than the women, who are addressed by their first names. In the academic context, both students and administrative staff are more likely to address a female professor by her first name and a male professor by his title. (Age is also a factor here, since female professors, on the whole, constitute a younger group than male professors.)

But the sexual politics of address terms is a complex issue. Is this non-parallel use of terms of address for women and men in the university necessarily unfavourable for women? If a female student or administrative staff member addresses a female professor by her first name, could this not express solidarity rather than lack of respect? Some feminist researchers (Tannen 1990a) maintain that women are less likely than men to be bothered by expressions of informality and may prefer less distancing terms of address. On the other hand, if a male student uses titles (*Professor* Hunter, *Dr.* Shore) to address his male professors, but then uses first names for his female professors, what does this difference reflect?

While various factors (status, solidarity, preference of addressee, familiarity of speakers) affect the choice of terms of address, the *systematic* use of non-parallel terms for women and men should be avoided. Such asymmetry usually disadvantages women. Once communication has been established, the use of familiar or formal terms of address can be negotiated on an individual basis.

Titles

In writing and in formal situations, people are often addressed by their title followed by their surname. Parallel terms of address for men and women should be used: a woman with a PhD should be addressed in the same way as a man with a PhD (*Professor* Joan Rosenberg / *Professor* John Rosenberg, *Doctor* Joan Rosenberg / *Doctor* John Rosenberg, *Dr.* Rosenberg). Never address female faculty members, in speech or writing, as *Ms, Miss,* or *Mrs.* if you address their male counterparts as *Dr.* or *Professor.*

The title *Ms* was popularized by feminists in the 1970s to replace *Miss* and *Mrs.* and provide a parallel term to *Mr.*, in that both designate gender without indicating marital status. Feminists advocate the use of *Ms* in order to keep private information (the presence or absence of a woman's relationship to a man) that is not relevant to work/formal situations. This decreases the harassment experienced by single women and also prevents the establishment of a hierarchy whereby married women are seen as more respectable and responsible. In short, eliminating *Mrs.* and *Miss* in favour of *Ms* allows women to be seen as people in their own right, rather than in relation to someone else (Miller and Swift 1976, 120).

Unfortunately, while *Ms* was intended to be the parallel term to *Mr.*, considerable evidence suggests that it is often not used in this way. Frank and Treichler (1989, 218) cite the following directive, sent to public information officers in the state of Pennsylvania: "If you use Ms. for a female, please indicate in parentheses after the Ms. whether it's Miss or Mrs."

David Graddol and Joan Swann (1989) report fairly extensive use of *Ms* in Britain: it seems to have replaced *Miss* in certain contexts as the title for unmarried women. Donna Atkinson (1987), in a Canadian study of attitudes towards the use of *Ms* and birthname retention among women, found that many of her respondents used three distinct forms: *Mrs.* (for married women), *Miss* (for women who had never been married), and *Ms* (for divorced women). These mis-uses of the neutral term *Ms* demonstrate the high premium placed on identifying women by their relationship (current or otherwise) to men.

In French, the distinction between *Madame* and *Mademoiselle* is based primarily on age, with older women generally referred to as *Madame* and younger women as *Mademoiselle*. Similar distinctions exist in German, Italian, and Spanish. The terms do not necessarily convey information about a woman's relationship to a man, as do *Mrs.* and *Miss*. However, an asymmetry is evident in these languages: each has only one title for men, which indicates neither marital status nor age.

The title *Madelle* was introduced in French to parallel *Monsieur*—much in the way *Ms* parallels *Mr.* in English—but its use has been very limited. Several groups advocate the use of *Madame* as the neutral term for women regardless of age or marital status. We advocate the use of *Madame* and *Mad.* as the parallel titles to *Monsieur. Mad.* is the abbreviation of *Madelle* and should be used only in written discourse.

In advocating the use of parallel titles for females and males, including *Ms* to replace *Mrs./Miss* and *Madame* and *Mad.* to replace *Madame/Mademoiselle*, we recognize that our recommendations may not take into consideration the particular concerns and experiences of all women. Frank and Treichler (1989, 216) report that "the rejection of the title *Mrs.* by white middle-class feminists is not necessarily shared by black women, who were traditionally denied the right to take their husband's names." Similarly, some lesbians, since most societies do not recognize marriages between two women, deliberately use the title *Miss* to signal that they have chosen not to marry men.

TERMS OF REFERENCE

While the terms of reference exemplified below serve both to define and to diminish women, the most serious example of sexism in the designation of women is no designation at all. Feminist literary critics have pointed to the absence of women writers from literary histories as a reflection of androcentric values. In writing this chapter, I was struck by the lack of references to female scholars, especially in academic journals of the 1950s, 1960s, and 1970s. Just as women writers are "lost" or "forgotten," so women scholars and researchers may be ignored or rendered invisible by a male-dominated society.

Names

Of the many differences in the ways women and men are referred to or designated, surnaming conventions are the most striking example of men's power to define women through naming. Spender (1985, 24–25) argues that the tradition of women taking their husband's surname upon marriage is "one more device for making women invisible" and subtly reinforces "the concept of women as the property of men." The problem is compounded when a woman is addressed by both the first name and surname of her husband (e.g., *Mrs. Stephen Brown*). Some women have broken with this tradition and have chosen to retain their own (or, at least, their father's) surname. Others, like artist Judy Chicago and scholar Julia Penelope, have completely dispensed with the patrilineal aspect of last names and taken the names of cities or of female friends or relatives. Cheris Kramarae, a well-known scholar in the area of language and gender, changed her name from "Kramer" (her husband's last name) to "Kramarae," in order to incorporate her mother's chosen name "Rae." Since 1979, women in Quebec legally have retained their surname upon marriage unless they make a special application to change it.

The academic context provides other examples of non-parallelism in the naming or designation of women and men. In academic discourse, female and male scholars and writers should be referred to in symmetrical ways. The designation of Virginia Woolf as *Mrs.* Woolf in the following passage contrasts sharply with the designation of male writers.

> "Quality" is the word to use here, for *Mrs. Woolf* was concerned less with projecting any given view of what is significant in experience than with the sort of thing, the moods, intuitions, blending of memories, sudden awarenesses of the symbolic in the real, that suggests how the inner life is really lived. The material environment, which she criticized *Bennett* and *Wells* and *Galsworthy* for concentrating on, was for her at most only a background. (Daiches 1970, 11)

Woolf's marital status is completely irrelevant to the concerns addressed in this passage, and her designation as a married woman diminishes her status as a professional writer. In a similar way, the media's asymmetrical references to public figures can detract from the professionalism of women: Mrs. Thatcher, Miss Navrativola as opposed to Mulroney, McEnroe.

Another type of asymmetry involves the use of women's first names. Women scholars are often designated by their first names and surnames, where comparable men are designated by their surnames only. Thus reference to sex is made when it is irrelevant. In some instances women are designated by only their first name. This was evident throughout the Canadian Liberal leadership convention in 1990, when the media often referred to the only female candidate, Sheila Copps, as "Sheila" while referring to male candidates such as Paul Martin and Jean Chrétien by their full names or surnames only. This difference can also be observed in many genres of fiction, where female characters are designated by first names and male characters by surnames:

> *Emily* felt the heat rise to her cheeks, and this brought further irritation. Anger at *Johnston*, but mostly at herself. (Barrett 1990, 414)

It is also to be found in academic prose. The following passage comes from a 1986 issue of the *Oxford Literary Review* on sexual difference:

> In Alice James's case, what is most striking is the relentless activity of the symptoms and of *Alice's* relationship to them—one which if it is not covered adequately by the category of the victim is no more satisfactorily met by the idea, expressed for example by her biographer Jean Strouse, that this illness was *Alice's* design and purpose in seeking compensation and attention from a restricted and restricting social world. *Alice's* experience—the range of that experience—hovers on an edge in which the lines between violence and the act are in their way as confused and troubling as that earlier example from *Masson*. (Rose 1986, 187)

In a context where there would be no confusion among the family members (Alice, Henry, and William James), Alice James is initially designated by her full name, but subsequent references use her first name only. In contrast, Jeffrey Masson is designated by his surname only. The impact of this difference can perhaps be seen more clearly if we consider substituting "Jeffrey" for "Masson." This informal designation would seem both unprofessional and condescending.♦ The familiar designation of Sheila Copps and Alice James in the above examples is demeaning and finds its parallel in the familiarity with which children and other marginalized individuals are addressed.

L a b e l s ▌

Like names and designations, the labels applied to women and women's work often diminish their value. Female and male political figures generally receive differing linguistic treatment in the press. On 13 July 1984, during Geraldine Ferraro's U.S. vice-presidential candidacy, the following appeared in *the Wall Street Journal* and the *Columbus Dispatch*, respectively (Geis 1987, 67).

> Mondale's Choice Rep. Ferraro, *Spunky* and Natural, Moves Into a Tougher League

> A *feisty* Ferraro challenged criticism that she doesn't have the experience to be Vice President, and then she challenged Vice President George Bush to a debate.

♦ Some feminist critics may use first names for women as a strategy for re-investing old usage with new meaning. However, here as elsewhere, it is essential to signal to the reader one's intentions.

Michael Geis points, in particular, to the use of *spunky* and *feisty* to describe Ferraro. Both words are normally reserved for individuals and animals that are not inherently potent or powerful. Geis comments (p. 68), "one can call a Pekinese dog spunky or feisty, but one would not, I think, call a Great Dane spunky or feisty." And the press would certainly not label George Bush, Ferraro's then opponent, as spunky or feisty. This differential linguistic treatment represents the woman as inherently powerless.

An article in the *Canadian Forum* described Sheila Copps's candidacy for the Liberal leadership in the following way:

> Although she is clearly starting well behind (both in terms of money and delegate base) she might very well be the Liberals' best bet. Young, articulate, fluently bilingual, an attractive *and* tough woman, she is out-spokenly and quite unashamedly on the left wing of the party. (Whitaker 1990, 14; emphasis in original)

The emphasized "*and*" seems to imply that a woman is not usually both attractive and tough. This is not a description one would expect to find applied to a male politician: firstly, his appearance would not be seen as relevant, and, secondly, the attribute *tough* would not typically be followed by the addition of *attractive*. Like the description of Ferraro, this representation of Copps throws into question the intrinsic potency of a female politician.

The French "women's" magazine, *Marie Claire*, published in its September 1989 issue an article, "Femmes de pouvoir," with the expressed purpose of describing "powerful" women. Yet the article describes professional women with a variety of adjectives that have nothing to do with their work or professions. The following example is symptomatic: "Nathalie Hocq. De Cartier en Poiray, cette jeune et pulpeuse pdg. roule sa bosse au royaume des bijoux" ("this young and voluptuous company president travels widely in the world of jewels"). The power and potency of this business woman is undermined by irrelevant references to her physical appearance.

In the academic context, women's writing and scholarship has often been labelled in a diminishing way. Sandra Gilbert and Susan Gubar (1979) cite the belittling descriptions that the poetry of Emily Dickinson and Elizabeth Barrett Browning has received from male readers and critics. Dickinson, for example, has been described in the following way:

> The woman poet as a type . . . makes flights into nature rather too easily and upon errands which do not have metaphysical importance enough to justify so radical a strategy. . . . Most probably [Dickinson's] poems would not have amounted to much if the author had not finally had her own romance, enabling her to fulfil herself like any other woman. (Ransom 1963, cited in Gilbert and Gubar 1979, xviii)

Women's scholarship continues to receive unflattering descriptions, often indirectly expressed. A prominent sociolinguist writes about the state of language and gender research (in the preface to a book on the topic, authored by a male academic):

> In the last two decades...there has been an enormous upsurge of interest, and literally thousands of papers and articles have been written on different aspects of the subject. Some have been insightful, informative, thought-provoking, scholarly and exciting. Very many of them have been none of these things. (Trudgill, 1985, ix)

Given that research on language and gender springs from the impetus of feminism and that most of the research is conducted by women academics, Trudgill's comment that much of this is not "insightful, informative, thought-provoking, scholarly and exciting" is an indirect attack on scholarship by women. He continues:

> In this pioneering work, Philip Smith takes a cool, careful look at all aspects of this research, adding a wealth of original data, insight and interpretation.

The use of the adjective "cool" to describe Smith's work suggests that other work on the topic has been something other than cool, perhaps emotional and irrational, adjectives stereotypically associated with women. The labelling of Smith's work as pioneering suggests that Smith breaks new ground in a way that his predecessors have failed to do. Thus Trudgill expands upon his negative characterization of women's scholarship.

Examples

Related to the problem of unfavourable labels for women is the negative characterization of women in illustrative material. Paula Treichler (1989) cites examples such as the use of "She made his life hell on earth" in a dictionary to illustrate the possible uses of the notion "hell." Linguistics and philosophical texts regularly use exemplary sentences, and the 1960s and 1970s provide all too many male-biased examples.

Many sentences very explicitly represent violence against women:

> Fred has been beating his wife.
> Fred stopped beating his wife.
> Fred hesitated to stop beating his wife.
> In one impulsive act, John picked Mary up and threw her on the bed.

Others simply reveal misogynist attitudes:

> *A girl by dating whom you are sure to catch a horrible disease.♦

Still others reinforce stereotypes regarding women and men's roles

> Mary cooked and cleaned.
> I like watching those girls crochet doilies.
> Harold's continuing fondling Astrid did not produce the desired results.
> Frankly, Merlin is a genius.
> Ramona, who frankly is a doll, is leaving.
> The fact that John flunked and Mary passed surprised Fred.

The examples below provide welcome relief from the conventional stereotypes illustrated above.

> She is as brilliant a woman as her mother.
> What her mother wants her to be is as strong a person as possible.
> What her mother wants her to be is such a fine surgeon that everyone will respect her.

♦ It is the convention in linguistic texts to mark ungrammatical sentences with an asterisk. Sentences are considered ungrammatical if they contain errors in sentence structure; asterisks are not related to content.

So eminent a scholar as Dr. Lucille Hein was here.
Mary's happy about her work, and John's happy about his children.✦

Materials for teaching language provide examples that are equally problematic in terms of the stereotypes that they reinforce. In an article, "Propositions pour une competence culturelle de l'enseignant et de l'apprenant," Pierre Trescases (1983) advocates the incorporation of sociocultural information into the teaching of basic French grammar. But the sample exercises he employs display males going to school and females staying at home. In other words, these are the sociocultural facts that are so important to convey to second-language learners of French.

Il va à la maternelle.	Elle habite dans une maison.
Il va au lycée.	Elle habite dans un appartement.
Il va à l'université.	Elle habite dans une villa.

GUIDELINES ▌

1. Use terms of address symmetrically.
   * Do not generally address female academics by their first names and their male counterparts by their titles. (Once communication is established, the individuals concerned can negotiate the use of familiar/formal address terms.)
   * Use *Ms Jones and Mr. Smith* rather than *Miss Jones and Mr. Smith*. In French, use *Madame Gervais and Monsieur Hulot* rather than *Mademoiselle Gervais and Monsieur Hulot*. (Use *Miss, Mrs.,* or *Mademoiselle* only if you know this to be the preferred title of the woman in question.)
   * If both individuals have doctorates, use *Dr. da Silva and Dr. Huang* or *Professor da Silva and Professor Huang* rather than *Ms da Silva and Dr. Huang*. In French, use *Professeur Poulin et Professeure Blanchard* or *Docteur Poulin et Docteure Blanchard* rather than *Professeur Poulin and Madame Blanchard*.
   * Use neutral terms such as *Ms* appropriately (equivalent to *Mr.*). Do not add *Miss* or *Mrs.* in brackets to convey marital status.

2. Do not assume that a married woman will have the same surname as her husband; some women choose not to take their husband's name on marriage. Only use a husband's surname for the wife if you know that is the name she has chosen to use.
3. Avoid the use of terms of endearment (*honey, sweetie, dear*) unless you are a personal friend. If you do not know the person's name, ask.
4. When writing to people whose individual names are unknown, use the following kinds of salutations:

English	French
To Whom it May Concern	A qui de droit
Dear Committee	Chers/Chères membres du comité
Dear Colleague	Cher/Chère collègue
Dear Registrar	Monsieur le Registraire/Madame la Registraire
Dear Chair/President	Monsieur le Directeur/Madame la Directrice
Dear Madam or Sir	Madame/Monsieur

✦ Examples are from *Linguistic Inquiry* 3–4 (1972), 3.

- Alternatively, use no salutation.
- For local written correspondence, telephone to determine the name of the person to whom you are writing.
- Using another form of correspondence (such as a memo to all concerned parties rather than a letter to each individual) can circumvent the problem.
5. When writing to a person whose sex is unknown:
   - If you have only initials preceding the surname, as in *J. A. Phipps*, begin the letter *Dear J. A. Phipps*.
   - If the first name is not gender-specific, as in *Chris Hatsfield*, begin the letter *Dear Chris Hatsfield*.
6. On forms, offer different titles (making sure that *Ms* is one of the options) and ask the individual to select the title by which s/he would prefer to be addressed. Many women prefer the term *birth name* to *maiden name*. Avoid the term *Christian name* as this introduces yet another form of bias.
7. Refer to females and males in a parallel manner.

> *Liberal leader* Jean Chrétien and *Ms* Audrey McLaughlin
> ➤ *Liberal leader* Jean Chrétien and *NDP leader* Audrey McLaughlin

> Judge Sopinka and *Madam* Wilson
> ➤ *Judges* Sopinka and Wilson

> *Mrs.* Woolf and Proust
> ➤ Woolf and Proust

> *Virginia* Woolf and Proust
> ➤ Woolf and Proust

8. Avoid labels that are demeaning to women or reinforce stereotypical images of women and men.

> The *brilliant linguist*, Noam, and *his attractive wife*, Carol Chomsky . . .
> ➤ The linguists, Carol Chomsky and Noam Chomsky . . .

F U R T H E R   R E A D I N G █

Francine Frank and Paula Treichler, *Language, Gender and Professional Writing* (New York: Modern Language Association, 1989).
♦ Provides a more detailed discussion of terms of reference in scholarly writing.

Sally McConnell-Ginet, "Address Forms in Sexual Politics" in *Women's Language and Style*, ed. Douglas Butturff and E. Epstein (Akron, OH: L and S Books, 1978).
♦ Contains further discussion of terms of address.

Una Stannard, *Mrs. Man* (San Francisco: Germainbooks, 1977).
♦ Contains a discussion of women's surnaming practices.

CHAPTER 8

NONSEXIST VISUAL IMAGES

Terry Lavender and Valerie Vanstone

A picture is worth more than 10 000 words.
Chinese proverb

In this chapter, we will show how gender bias distorts the way women are presented in printed images. We will then suggest ways to eliminate this bias, both in the content and the use of images.

Often we skim over the images in publications, not even noticing how women in those images are presented. Yet most of the women—and in some cases there are none—will be diminished or limited in some way. These images become part of a woman's conception of herself and influence how she feels about her own status and abilities (Butler and Paisley 1980, 49–50). They also persuade the male viewer that his social dominance is justified.

IMAGES: WHAT THEY ARE, HOW THEY WORK

For the purposes of this chapter, the word *images* means the pictures reproduced in editorial and advertising print materials, such as newspapers, periodicals, brochures, and posters, as well as those in educational materials, such as slides, filmclips, and textbooks. Images may be commissioned photographs or illustrations, or they may be public-domain or stock art.

In advertisers' terms, a "good image" is one that draws the viewer's attention and associates a product or service with promises of success, comfort, sexual satisfaction, or power (Dyer 1988, 96). In non-advertising material, a "good image" is one that illustrates a point, tells a story, conveys emotion, and includes interesting

le and situations. Sometimes images are used simply to break up a long block
of text.

But at the same time, images have an impact beyond the surface message they
convey. Images, more than language, tell us who we are and who we should aspire
to be. Consider, for example, slides used in an architecture class to show the inside
of a particular building and that feature users of that building. If all the women
shown are secretaries or receptionists and the men are executives, then the slides
send a definite message about the relative position of women and men in society.

Unlike written language, which requires the reader's conscious attention,
images can exercise their effect passively. You do not have to concentrate on an
image to be affected by it. And while many people are becoming critical "con-
sumers" of language, fewer realize how images and the image business work.

GENDER BIAS IN PRINT IMAGES

Print images treat women in three ways. Women can be forgotten, objectified, or
treated as individual human beings.

Firstly, women are most often forgotten entirely. If included, they are often
diminished in some way, treated as less important or less interesting than other
subjects (men, animals, cars, buildings). Women can be forgotten or diminished
in the *number* of images, the *content* of the images, and in the *treatment* (size and
placement) of the images on the page. The message is, women were at the event,
but they're not really important so we can leave them out. Or, women are involved
in this activity, but they couldn't be as good as men, so we'll leave them out. Or
women are involved, but we forgot to get photos of them. Sometimes, images of
women are used only to illustrate so-called "women's issues."

Women can be forgotten in several ways:

- they can be left out entirely (this can follow naturally when women are omitted
  from the text);
- they can be relegated to the back of a publication or to the inside (gutter) or the
  bottom of the page;
- they can be given less prominence in a publication or unequal treatment within
  the same story;
- they can be given less space or only occasional space in a periodical publication.

Secondly, women in images are often objectified or limited in some way—
stereotyped, idealized, sentimentalized, or used as decoration. The message in
such images is that women are not fully human, so it is alright to reduce them to
body parts or objects of humour or to use them to promote a product or a program.
Women can be objectified in both the content and treatment of the image.

Women are objectified in several ways:

- they are not complete people;
- they are reduced to body parts;
- they are not related to the main subject of the story or image;
- their faces and bodies are airbrushed and stylized;
- they are portrayed as idealized, unattainable;
- there is an additional, hidden agenda in the narrative or action of the image
  (such as hostility hidden in humour).

SUMMER BLOCKBUSTERS
MOVIES
A GUIDE TO THIS SUMMER'S HOTTEST MOVIES
BY REED FORSTER

DICK TRACY An all-star cast brings the square-jawed crime fighter to the screens. Stars Warren Beatty in the title role, Madonna, Charles Durning and Dick Van Dyke. Dir. Warren Beatty. June 15.

ROBOCOP 2 In the Detroit of the future, Robocop Murphy struggles to recover his human past as he battles a drug-crazed gang, resists mind control rehabilitation by a OCP official, and finally joins forces with his partner to battle a terrifying robot created by OCP to replace him. Stars Peter Weller and Nancy Allen. Dir. Irvin Kershner. June 22.

NAVY SEALS An elite naval combat and rescue team must destroy American Stinger missiles that have fallen into the hands of Islamic terrorists. Stars Charlie Sheen and Michael Biehn. Dir. Lewis Teague. July.

Tom Cruise in Days of Thunder.

DAYS OF THUNDER Tom Cruise is an ambitious young NASCAR race driver teamed up with Robert Duvall, a legendary crew chief and a genius at building cars. Dir. Tony Scott. June 27.

MEN AT WORK Brothers Charlie Sheen and Emilio Estevez are two garbage men who uncover the body of a City Commissioner, are chased by underworld goons, encounter a little romance and try to track down the killer so they can clear their names. Written and directed by Emilio Estevez.

MY BLUE HEAVEN Steve Martin is a smooth New York gangster scheduled to testify against a well-known mobster. To protect him, the government ships him to a sleepy town in California. Unimpressed by the boring town, Martin decides to add a little 'excitement' much to the chagrin of Rick Moranis, the FBI agent assigned to protect him. Dir. Herbert Ross. Aug.

YOUNG GUNS II Emilio Estevez returns as Billy the Kid and reunites with his former band (Kiefer Sutherland, Lou Diamond Phillips) to battle corrupt politicians. Also stars Christian Slater and William L. Peterson. Dir. Geoff Murphy. Aug. 1.

The cast of Young Guns II

QUIGLEY DOWN UNDER In turn-of-the-century Australia, Tom Selleck is a sharpshooting American cowboy hired by a wealthy Australian rancher to rid his land of wild dingos. Upon arriving down under though, Selleck finds out the rancher has other plans for him. Dir. Simon Wincer. Aug.

DIVE The U.S. sub Standard sets sail on its maiden voyage with bumbling, claustrophobic Captain Biff Banner (Bill Pullman). Dir. Mark W. Travis. Aug.

GREMLINS 2 Gizmo the Mogwai hooks up with much of the original cast again to spawn a new generation of gremlins. Dir. Joe Dante. June 15.

DUCKTAILS Scrooge McDuck and his three nephews, Huey, Dewey and Louie, search for buried treasure and uncover a magic lantern, complete with genie. Aug. 3.

MO' BETTER BLUES Spike Lee writes, produces, directs and co-stars in this contemporary look at the life of a New York trumpet player forced to choose between his music and his women. Also stars Denzel Washington. Aug. 3.

Jack Nicholson directs and stars in The Two Jakes.

THE TWO JAKES Jack Nicholson reprises his role as Jake Gittes from Chinatown. It's 11 years later and Gittes is investigating a killing in '40s L.A. when he discovers connections to a deadly course of events from his past. Dir. Jack Nicholson. Aug. 10.

GRAFFITI BRIDGE Prince stars, writes and directs the story about two people who are involved in a power struggle over a nightclub they co-own. Money rules the world of sleazy Morris E. Day while Prince is driven by a deeper force expressed through the powerful energy and raw beauty of his music. Aug.

BETSY'S WEDDING Eager to give his daughter the perfect wedding, Alan Alda agrees to join in one of his double-dealing brother-in-law's shady schemes. When their plan goes awry, it looks as though Daddy will be in jail rather than giving his daughter away. Dir. Alan Alda. June 22.

THE JUNGLE BOOK Disney's classic animated rendition of Rudyard Kipling's tale of Mowgli, the boy raised by a wolf pack. July 13.

ARACHNOPHOBIA A highly poisonous South American spider makes his home in a small Californian town and puts the bite on everyone around. Stars Jeff Daniels, Julian Sands and John Goodman. Dir. Frank Marshall. July 20.

TAKING CARE OF BUSINESS An upwardly mobile executive's filofax is found by an inmate on 'temporary leave' from his minimum security prison. The jailbird assumes the executive's identity, tries to

Mel Gibson in Air America.

DIE HARD 2 Bruce Willis returns as detective John McClane but this time he plays cat-and-mouse with an elite special forces unit that has seized a major airport. Dir. Renny Harlin. July 4.

AIR AMERICA Mel Gibson and Robert Downey Jr. are pilots during the Vietnam war involved in the secret bombing missions. Dir. Roger Spottiswoode. Aug 10.

EXORCIST III This instalment picks up where the first left, the demon has possessed a young priest and now is free to roam from body to body. Stars George C. Scott. Dir. William Peter Blatty. Aug.

THE ADVENTURES OF FORD FAIRLANE Andrew Dice Clay stars as an unorthodox private investigator specializing in the music industry world. Dir. Renny Harlin. July 13.

FLIGHT OF THE INTRUDER Too many missions with too little purpose and the death of his flying partner prompt a pilot and his new bombardier to conduct an unauthorized mission deep behind enemy lines. The flight—a bombing raid on a missile depot in Hanoi—bring their personal code of honour into conflict with their commitment to serve as ordered. Star Danny Glover, Willem Dafoe and Brad Johnson. Dir. John Milius.

collect the $1,000 reward for the return of the filofax, see a World Series game and sneak back into prison, all before they notice he's escaped. Stars James Belushi and Charles Grodin. Dir. Arthur Hiller. Aug. 17.

GHOST DAD Bill Cosby stars as a father who doesn't let dying get in the way of developing a continuing relationship with his kids. Dir. Sidney Poitier. June 29.

JETSONS The cartoon family hits the big screen. The Jetsons move to a new planet and find themselves caught in a battle between the ecology and the forces of technology. July 6.

PROBLEM CHILD John Ritters stars in this comedy about an unsuspecting suburban couple who adopt a seemingly lovable child who wreaks havoc on their household. Dir. Dennis Dugan. July 27.

Animated nuclear family The Jetsons.

GHOST Stranded as a ghost in New York city, Patrick Swayze is determined to communicate with Demi Moore, the woman he loves. Dir. Jerry Zucker. July 27.

THE FRESHMAN Film student Matthew Broderick's college career is altered when he is befriended by Marlon Brando, a genial father figure who also is an organized crime boss with an eligible daughter. Dir. Andrew Bergman. Aug. 17.

PLATLINERS Five ambitious medical students embark on a chilling life-after-death experiment. Stars Kiefer Sutherland, Julia Roberts and Kevin Bacon. Dir. Joel Schumacher. June 29.

QUICK CHANGE Bill Murray, Geena Davis and Randy Quaid star as a trio of fed-up New Yorkers who make a foray into crime. Dir. Joel Schumacher. June 29.

Director Spike Lee.

PRESUMED INNOCENT Harrison Ford is a prosecuting attorney assigned to investigate the murder of a beautiful colleague with whom he has been having a torrid extramarital affair. Soon, he finds that he himself is a suspect in the case. Also stars Brian Dennehy and Raul Julia. Dir. Alan J. Pakula. July 20.

Peter Weller is Robocop in Robocop II.

Forgotten women: This entertainment page from a weekly tabloid suggests that only men and robots direct or star in movies. There are only two females on the page: beautiful, stereotyped, and minuscule, the cartoon Jetsons.

Thirdly, and only rarely, women are presented as complete human beings, living real lives. The message in such images is that women, like men, deserve to be taken seriously as persons. Both the content of the images and the way they are presented will show respect for and interest in women as subjects.

Diversity is one of the hallmarks of presenting women as complete human beings. The women portrayed should include all sizes, ages, shapes, and races. Women should not be portrayed in stereotyped situations or roles. They should be shown as active, as capable of self-expression, and in control of the situation. Another key is that the images of women should have a real function on the page. They should impart information and not merely serve as decoration. Their use should have "story value," not "object value."

Ways of giving women equal representation include:

- featuring them as often as male subjects;
- giving them equal space;
- giving them equal treatment;
- giving them respectful treatment (not trivializing them or making them the butt of humour).

CHECKING FOR GENDER BIAS

There are three main criteria for assessing the differing treatment of men and women in images: the number, treatment, and content of images.

- Number: How many images of women appear in comparison to images of men and other subjects?
- Treatment (size and placement): What kind of emphasis is the image given?
- Content: What is included inside the frame of the image (subject, background, action, emotion)?

Number and treatment

Studies of reader behaviour tell the publishing industry which pages, and which areas of each page, capture readers' attention. This information governs how advertisers purchase space and how editors place their headlines, stories, and images for greatest "readability." Advertisers calculate which position on the page will give their product the most immediate and repeated exposure.

Research (Nelson 1983, 149) shows that the most advantageous position, in terms of reader exposure, is on the front or the back cover. For broadsheet newspapers (folded horizontally), an image placed above the fold gets more exposure than one below the fold.

A reader casually flipping through a publication first notices images on the outside of the page. Images on the inside near the gutter (the blank space between two facing pages) receive least exposure, especially if they are also close to the bottom of the page (Nelson 1983, 141–42).

The first step in identifying the degree of gender bias in images is to analyse the number and treatment (size and placement) of the images. Figure 1 is a sample form, which may be copied.

Count each time a woman, man, or other type of subject (animal/thing/scene) appears. For example, for a photograph showing two men, one woman, and a horse, you would count one female subject, two male subjects, and one "other."

SCIENCE-INTER

PAR SOPHIE MALAVOY

DÉCLOISONNONS LES SCIENCES SOCIALES

Les unités de sciences sociales doivent décloisonner leurs programmes de premier cycle, les revoir en mettant l'accent sur la formation générale des étudiants et se soucier de l'intégration socioprofessionnelle de leurs diplômés. C'est là l'une des 44 recommandations du rapport remis au Conseil des universités, en novembre dernier, par le Comité d'étude sectorielle en sciences sociales. Ce comité était présidé par Louis Maheu, de l'Université de Montréal.

La révision des programmes de premier cycle doit viser, selon le comité, à renforcer « les capacités d'analyse et de synthèse, de calcul et d'expression écrite, de jugement pratique et de communica-tion interpersonnelle ; l'approfondisse-ment des connaissances par l'initiation aux fondements d'une discipline ou d'un champ d'études ; l'élargissement des connaissances et le développement de l'esprit critique par le contact avec le mode de pensée d'autres disciplines que celles de la concentration, en n'excluant pas celles situées hors du champ général des sciences humaines. » Pour qu'on puisse atteindre ces buts, les étudiants devraient suivre au moins le tiers de leurs cours en dehors de leur discipline.

De plus, une priorité accrue doit être accordée à la mise au point de cours fondamentaux par les professeurs les plus expérimentés.

Source

LACHANCE, F. « Le rapport Maheu préconise l'ouver-ture des programmes de premier cycle en sciences socia-les », *Forum*, 20 novembre 1989.

LES PRIX DU QUÉBEC 1989

Gérard Bergeron

Jacques Leblanc

Les plus hautes distinctions accordées par le gouvernement du Québec dans les domaines des sciences humaines et des sciences de la nature, soit le prix Léon-Gérin et le prix Marie-Victorin, ont été décernées respectivement cette année au politicologue Gérard Bergeron et au physiologiste Jacques Leblanc.

Gérard Bergeron est l'un des pères de la science politique au Québec. Il est l'au-teur d'une vingtaine de livres et de centai-nes d'articles sur la théorie politique, sur la politique internationale et sur les rap-ports Québec-Canada. Ancien professeur

à l'Université Laval, il est depuis le début des années 80 attaché à l'École d'admi-nistration publique.

De son côté, Jacques Leblanc, profes-seur à l'Université Laval, jouit d'une réputation internationale pour ses recher-ches sur l'adaptation de l'être humain au froid. Il s'est aussi illustré en physiologie du travail et de l'exercice physique, en nutrition et en endocrinologie, comme en témoignent plus de 200 publications scientifiques et au-delà de 150 conféren-ces données à travers le monde.

FERNANDE SAINT-MARTIN REMPORTE LE PRIX MOLSON 1989

Madame Fernande Saint-Martin, pro-fesseure à l'Université du Québec à Montréal, a reçu en novembre dernier le prix Molson 1989 pour les sciences humaines du Conseil des arts du Canada.

Écrivaine, muséologue, chercheuse et professeure à l'Université du Québec à Montréal, Fernande Saint-Martin a joué un rôle de premier plan autant dans l'avancement de la cause des femmes que dans la diffusion des arts au Québec. Elle a, entre autres, mis sur pied en 1960 l'édition française de la revue *Châtelaine* et dirigé le Musée d'art contemporain de Montréal de 1972 à 1977.

Fernande Saint-Martin a mérité de nombreux prix tout au long de sa carrière dont le prix André-Laurendeau 1988 décerné par l'Acfas.

LE CANADA À LA RESCOUSSE DE L'EVEREST

Grâce à une subvention de 229 000 $ du Centre de recherches pour le dévelop-pement international (CRDI), des cher-cheurs népalais et chinois conjugueront leurs efforts afin de préparer la création

Equal treatment in magazine layout: The woman's photo runs in the inside column, but at the top of the page and the same size as those of the two men. All three subjects are backlit, cropped to the head and shoulders, over thirty, and have pleasant, unglamorous faces. Why are gender-balanced layouts like this so rare?

Figure 1
Number, size, and placement analysis form

Publication title: _____

Publication date(s): _____

	Total number of images	Women		Men		Other	
		Number	% of total	Number	% of total	Number	% of total
Feature treatment *(front or back page; 2- or 3-column; top/outside of page)*							
Non-feature treatment *(1-column; inside and bottom of page)*							
Total							

Count pictures of crowd scenes and people of indeterminate sex (such as babies) as "other." Decide whether the images receive "feature" treatment or not. (Is the image on the front page of the publication? How large is it? Is it near the top of the page?) Compare the percentage of images of women that receive feature treatment to the percentage of images of men that receive such treatment. For periodical publications, consider several issues (four issues of a quarterly or seven issues of a daily newspaper, for example).

Content

The number and treatment of images are just two indicators of gender bias. The content of images also must be considered. A tabloid newspaper's "Sunshine Girl" passes the number (every issue), size (full-page), and placement (page 3) tests, but few would claim it is a positive representation of women.

Because of their frequency and visual impact, advertising images of women are among the most powerful we encounter. North American English-language advertising appeals to the heterosexual white male's fantasy of the ideal woman. Women's poses, bodies, and smiles are used to add mystery and sex to products or services. "Women are depicted in a quite different way from men—not because the feminine is different from the masculine—but because the 'ideal' spectator is always assumed to be male and the image of the woman is designed to flatter him" (Berger 1972, 64). Most designers and artists have trained in this advertising tradition, and many editors take their cue from advertising in their choice of editorial images. Quebec-trained designers and graphic artists appear to reflect a social and cultural milieu that is more inclusive of women.

Because advertising has such a profound influence on editorial communication, it is useful to look at how women are treated in advertising images. There is no doubt that advertising relies on sexist imagery, and several studies over the past twenty years have proposed ways to identify the type and degree of gender bias in advertising.[✦] One system that has been adopted by many researchers is the "level of consciousness" scale devised by Suzanne Pingree, Robert Hawkins, Matilda Butler, and William Paisley. Pingree divided images of women into five categories:

- Level 1: Woman is a two-dimensional, non-thinking decoration; she is objectified.
- Level 2: Woman's place is in the home or in womanly (nurse, secretary) occupations; she is a stereotype.
- Level 3: Woman may be a professional but her first place is in the home; she is inferior.
- Level 4: Women and men must be equals.
- Level 5: Women and men are individuals (Barnes 1984, 46).

Today, as in 1974 when the Pingree scale was published, examples of levels 1 through 3 are more easily found than examples of level 5. Beer commercials showing women as "la goddess," "fox," or even "la artsy type" are at level 1. A television ad depicting a harried housewife trying to find a tasty microwave chicken to appease her hungry family is level 2.

This scale can be readily adapted to non-advertising images. The "Sunshine Girl," for example, would be a level 1 image: woman as decoration. A poster

---

✦ For example, Goffman 1987; Courtney and Whipple 1983; Barnes 1984.

campaign that features a smiling model posing with a microscope to encourage high school girls to take science programs is also at level 1 and will probably not achieve its purpose—though it may increase the number of males in the program. A photo essay about a surgeon that depicts her getting dinner for her family and cleaning the house as well as performing surgery would be level 3. Level 4 images may be formulaic and therefore unnatural. Obviously, there is no formula for level 5 images.

Figure 2 is designed to identify gender bias in the content of images. For periodicals and newspapers, it is best to sample several issues of the publication.

ELIMINATING GENDER BIAS: A USERS' GUIDE

We are used to relating to men's emotions, actions, and stories in published images, because they are what most publications show us. If we are not used to recognizing women's emotions, actions, and stories, it is because editors and designers are not giving them equal space and fair treatment.

FIGURE 2

Content analysis form

Publication title: _____

Publication date(s): _____

Level	Number	Percentages of total
1		
2		
3		
4		
5		
Total		

It takes time to educate designers, editors, illustrators, and photographers. It takes money to ensure equal numbers of good quality images of both men and women. It takes effort to produce nonsexist images, because it means examining each image in a new light. It means not automatically accepting the cliché that has worked before. It means becoming aware.

Working with designers, photographers, and artists

Using cliché images from the media and advertising industry is easier for editors, artists, and photographers who are under pressure, over budget, and worried about deadlines. Most of the time, the choice is an unconscious one. The biased image simply feels familiar; it feels right.

Illustrators, designers, and photographers should not be contracted until it is clear that they fit the needs of the publication. Samples of their work should be reviewed and the requirements of the project in question explained. An artist should always supply rough and intermediate sketches; a photographer, contact sheets. Photographers who show little understanding of non-biased images should be accompanied on the shoot by someone who understands the assignment. After the photos are taken, it may be too late, and it definitely costs money to replace a biased image.

Technical and artistic considerations should never outweigh gender bias in the choice of which image to run. Choosing between a sexist and a nonsexist photo, for example, the editor may prefer the biased image because the framing, exposure, or focus is better. But technical flaws are fixable, as the advertising industry knows. Photographs can be corrected in the darkroom, on the designer's screen, or at the film house. Illustrations can be redrawn or retouched. The question becomes, do you spend the time and money necessary to correct the technical flaws in an unbiased image if that is all you have to work with?

Illustrations in the Quebec-based science magazine Interface *consistently present men and women as equal partners in the excitment and tribulations of scientific research.*

Building a nonsexist photo library

In-house publications, such as employee newsletters and campus newspapers, usually stress the human element in their stories—long-serving employees, professors conducting research, and so on. To illustrate these stories the publications often depend on the story subjects supplying photos. If the editors and art directors of these publications did a check of their photo files they would probably find a lot more images of male subjects than female subjects.

Editors can remedy this by taking the time to commission or shoot photographs of the women as well as the men in their organizations. Often it is best to arrange for photos before a story is completed. Some women have found it useful to have black and white photos taken and sent to the in-house publication for its photo files. The photo should be updated every few years.

Visual images in the classroom

Guidelines for choosing editorial and advertising images apply equally well to choosing instructional aids such as slides and filmclips.

In all disciplines, instructors should vary their choice of classroom images to include women and to present them in a positive way. Historical biases should not be presented without comment: an art class on the European nude, for example, needs some explanation of the context of male patronage that dictated its conventions. Anatomy posters should feature both male and female bodies.

Slide collections and posters produced by educational supply companies and schoolboards may reflect an out-of-date, biased attitude towards women and should be carefully screened for gender bias.

This advertisement for scientific "big brothers" and "big sisters" is a good example of gender-inclusive text and images.

EXCUSES, EXCUSES

Editors find many excuses for using biased images. See if some of these sound familiar.

"No one sent me the schedule for the women's teams, so I couldn't assign a photographer."
A good editor develops good networks, with female as well as male coaches, athletes, and managers. It might help to remember that women are used to being shut out by sports desks. In general, their publicity budgets are also lower than men's. And don't be surprised if they sometimes make the tactical decision not to approach a publication that has ignored or insulted them in the past.

"Women's sports are boring."
Look again.

Images of female athletes showing speed, aggressiveness, and skill are still unusual in the mass media. This photo of teenage all-stars in an exhibition tournament received feature treatment in a major newspaper. The event was well marketed, and the photographer was assigned to take action shots.

"It's not my job to ensure equal coverage."
Let's look at this a different way. If half your potential readers are women, are you doing your job if you publish only images of men? And if it's not your job, whose job is it?

"Only X% of our readers are women."
Your female readership may be small because they cannot find anything to relate to in your publication.

"What's wrong with a photo of an attractive female?"
Nothing, if it also has news or information value. Is "attractive female" your first, or only, criterion for choosing a particular image?

"What's wrong with running a humorous photo of a woman?"
Hostility often masquerades as humour. Do you apply the same sense of humour to images of men? Are the images of women in your publication humorous, or belittling?

"The photo we ran may have been biased, but technically it was a better shot."
Black and white negatives are forgiving. Problems in exposure and framing can be fixed in the darkroom and with good cropping.

"We're giving the readers what they want."
Are you really? Which readers? How do you know? A reader survey on photo content and treatment might show otherwise.

"It's not my fault if the woman in this photo looks coy, seductive, dumb . . . . That's how she looks."
Check your contact sheets and talk to your photographer. The photographer is always in charge of, and responsible for, the photo situation. The use of light, the angle of the shot, directions to the subject, and the decision when to expose each frame determine the final image. Women themselves may believe they are supposed to look coy or seductive, since that has been their role model for several centuries. A photographer who waits until a male subject reveals his true self, may be satisfied with a female subject who offers a pleasing female stereotype. If a female subject adopts a stereotypic pose or expression, the photographer is in the best position to recognize and correct it.

CHECKLISTS: RECOGNIZING GENDER BIAS

1. Forgotten women
   - Are women left out entirely?
   - Are women relegated to inferior positions in the publication?
   - Are women given less space?
   - Are the women who appear token women?

2. Objectified women
   - Are the women in the images stereotypes?
   - Are they used as decorative objects?
   - Are the women idealized images?
   - Are they objects of humour?

3. Women as people
   - Do the images include women of all ages, sizes, shapes, and races?
   - Do the women in the images relate to the story?
   - Do women appear as often as men?

SCIENCE

ave buoys up float firm

de reusable
ve process

puff up. The swelling beads fill the interior space, squeezing together into a solid lightweight plastic-foam core. If the float's shell is pierced later by a rock or a sharp-prowed boat, it could take weeks for enough water to seep into the foam core to spoil its buoyancy.

You need those foam-plastic cores in your floats, says Svirklys, to be certified for sales in the U.S. And this had created an environmental issue. Domal used to make its cores from beads of polyurethane. That process used chlorofluorocarbons (CFCs) to puff up the beads, once they were inside the box. But CFCs came to be seen as a threat to the planet's protective high-altitude ozone layer, and industry everywhere was asked to stop using them.

Svirklys and company turned to Ortech International, the big research centre in Mississauga. Could it help?

Yes it could, and more than he expected. Steven Nazar, manager of Ortech's plastics technology division, proposed switching the core material from polyurethane to polystyrene beads.

Nazar knew the old polyurethane was a thermoset material. Like the stuff used for pot handles and kitchen counter surfaces, it can be heated and molded but hardens permanently into its final shape. It could never be melted and remolded later. If anyone tried that, the stuff would simply char, and maybe give off a few nasty gases such as cyanide.

Nazar also knew that polystyrene was a thermoplastic material, part of a very different family that could be melted and molded again and again. Thermoplastics are used in both foam and clear plastic coffee cups, in some carpet fibres, in garbage bags, in lots of things.

The problem was, other marine-float makers had used polystyrene for their foam cores and it did not puff up so well. They had bought the stuff in the form of beads that were already fluffed up a bit, so they had air bubbles in them. These semi-fluffed beads were put in the float cases and heated to make them fluff up bigger. Steam was good for this, so the other makers had stuck a steam pipe into each float case and wiggled it around among the beads. Generally, not every bead got the same blast of steam and the puffing was uneven.

BIG EDGE: Ortech chemist Steven Nazar, left, came up with idea for new dock float, top, that could give the Scarborough company more than 10 per cent of the world market.

make the water boil. That's the way microwave ovens get food hot enough to cook, by boiling the water molecules that are scattered through the food's structure. In this case, the mi-

enough to be soft enough to expand ideally.

Ortech had another simple answer. A little salt was added to the water sprayed on the beads. Salt water boils at a higher temperature than ordinary water. Presto: The steam, inside the floats, in the oven, was hotter than 103 degrees and the beads turned very soft and puffed up, as Nazar puts it, "like popcorn".

This may not sound very complex but it seems no one had thought of doing it before, which was why his Ortech contract got Svirklys a patent on the idea of treating plastics with microwaves. Now if the idea spreads, the Scarborough firm may have whole new markets opening for it.

Cheesecake on the science page? Layouts like this can happen when the editor is short of good visuals. The pictures are publicity photos supplied by the company that sells the invention in the story. The man is identified as the scientist who conceived the idea. The woman's presence is unexplained. She is, in fact, an advertising cliché—a languid female body; sexualized by nudity, camera angle, and lighting; her presence gratuitous except to draw attention to the product. Yet her photo is larger than the other two photos combined.

- Are they given equal space and equal treatment?
- Are they treated with respect?
- Are they active—operating machinery, teaching, conducting experiments, competing at sports?

Checklist for editors/designers

Overall considerations

- Do you run equal numbers of images of women and men?
- Do you feature women on covers and in feature sections as often as men?
- Does the way you size, crop, caption, and lay out images result in equal treatment for male and female subjects?
- Do the images you run present women as real people, not fantasies, stereotypes, or clowns?
- Do your cartoon strips depict female characters equally and fairly?
- Do you assign photographers to events involving women?
- Do you select photos of women for their story value?
- Are you aware of advertising and media clichés and do you avoid them?
- Are you active in commissioning and using nonsexist images?
- Do you run only non-biased images?

Working with photographers and illustrators

- Do you check for gender bias in their portfolio and ask what they know about sexism?
- Do you specify clearly that your contract with them demands non-biased images?
- Do you ask photographers to provide contact sheets, and illustrators to provide rough sketches, so gender bias can be eliminated early in the project?
- Do you go with a photographer to the photo shoot if you have any doubts about their bias?
- Do you respect their professionalism while insisting on bias-free images?

Checklist for women photo subjects: working with photographers

- Do you expect respectful treatment during the photo session?
- Are you aware of clichés and stereotypes applied to female photo subjects and do you avoid them?
- Do you ask to see a contact sheet and request a say in the final choice of the image if you have any doubts about the photographer's understanding of bias?
- Are you prepared for photo requests? Do you have photos done ahead of time and keep them on file?
- Do you know if your office or department has a communications/public relations budget and if it is being used to promote women's images equally?

Checklist for photographers

- Do you set up your shots to avoid female stereotypes and advertising clichés?
- Do you expect female subjects to be as varied and surprising as male subjects?
- Do you actually "see" the female subjects involved in a photo opportunity?
- Do you look for a shot where female subjects are in the centre of the action?
- Do you shoot athletes or politicians similarly, regardless of whether they are female or male?

Checklist for illustrators

- Do your cartoon strips and illustrations feature female characters in a variety of roles?
- Do your standing illustrations (e.g., in banners, mastheads) avoid stereotypes of women?
- Do you avoid presenting clichés of women for "humorous" effect (e.g., prim librarian, dumb blonde, harried housewife, marriage-hungry spinster)?

Checklist for classroom instructors

- Do you choose textbooks that have been edited for gender bias?
- Do you illustrate your lectures with images of women as well as men?
- Do you use slides and other visuals that show women as real people?
- Do you avoid dated, gender-biased films, slides, and posters?
- Are you active in producing and selecting nonsexist images?
- Do you preface a presentation of biased images with a discussion of the historical context that produced them?

FURTHER READING

Adbusters Quarterly. Vancouver: Adbusters Media Foundation.
♦ This publication provides a sceptical analysis of print and broadcast advertising and offers free materials and strategies for lobbying for change.

John Berger, et al., eds., *Ways of Seeing* (London: Penguin, 1972).
♦ A good and amply illustrated introduction to the meaning and effect of images.

Matilda Butler and William Paisley, *Women and the Mass Media* (New York: Human Sciences Press, 1980).
♦ The chapter "Sexism in Image" provides specific material on the treatment of women.

Alice E. Courtney and Thomas W. Whipple, *Sex Stereotyping in Advertising* (Lexington, MA: Lexington Books, 1983).
♦ Provides a theoretical look at the subject.

Creative Source (Toronto: Wilcord Publications, 1990).
♦ An annual guide to Canadian illustrators, designers, photographers, and stock art suppliers, including some samples of work.

Gillian Dyer, *Advertising as Communication* (London: Routledge, 1988).
♦ A good introduction, with a chapter on the use of visual images in general.

Erving Goffman, *Gender Advertisements* (New York: Harper and Row, 1987).
♦ Categorizes the kinds of images of women in advertising, with many examples.

E.H. Gombrich, "The Visual Image" in *Communication* (San Francisco: W.H. Freeman, 1972).
♦ An overview of communications technology.

Guidelines for Bias-Free Publishing (Hightown, NJ: McGraw-Hill, n.d.).
♦ Offers advice on recognizing and eliminating gender bias in visual images.

Jean Kilbourne, *Killing Us Softly: Advertising Images of Women* (Cambridge, MA: Cambridge Documentary Films, 1979).
Jean Kilbourne, *Still Killing Us Softly* (Cambridge, MA: Cambridge Documentary Films, 1987).
♦ Two films that are powerful indictments of the treatment of women by advertisers.

Rhonda Lee, ed., *Guide to Nonsexist Language and Visuals* (Madison, WI: University of Wisconsin, 1985).
♦ Offers advice on recognizing and eliminating gender bias in visual images.

Roy Paul Nelson, *Publication Design*, 3rd ed. (Dubusque, IO: Wm. C. Brown, 1983).
♦ Provides information regarding the mechanics of creating, choosing, and printing images.

New Vision Technologies, *Presentation Task Force. Computer Clip Art* (Nepean, ON, 1990).
♦ Provides non-biased computer clip art.

Judy Pickens, *The Copy-to-Press Handbook* (New York: John Wiley and Sons, 1985).
♦ Provides information regarding the mechanics of creating, choosing, and printing images.

Charles J. Tannen, ed., *A Handbook of Magazine Publishing*, 2nd ed. (New Canaan, CT: Folio Publishing, 1983).
♦ Provides information regarding the mechanics of creating, choosing, and printing images.

Gaye Tuchman, Arlene Kaplan Daniels, and James Benet, eds., *Hearth and Home: Images of Women in the Mass Media* (New York: Oxford University Press, 1978).
♦ "The Image of Woman in Advertising" by Lucy Komisar and "The Image of Woman in Textbooks" by Marjorie B. U'Ren are especially worthwhile.

Implementing Reform:

Social and Political

Considerations

Susan Ehrlich and Ruth King

LANGUAGE REFORM AND SOCIAL CHANGE

9

While many feminist theorists see discriminatory language as contributing to the construction and maintenance of sexual inequalities, others view language as being merely symptomatic of such inequalities. According to the language-as-symptom view, as soon as we have put an end to discriminatory attitudes, our language use will change and discriminatory language will disappear.

Those who subscribe to the language-as-symptom view tend also to believe that the "idea that one can change people's attitude toward women through linguistic action is very naive. It is quite the reverse—how we refer to women will change as and when attitudes toward women change" (Geis 1987, 6). Underlying Geis' comment are two assumptions: (1) that language is a relatively neutral and transparent means of representing reality and (2) that language does not influence social behaviour but simply responds to changing social realities.

In arguing for the necessity of language reform, feminists have questioned both of these assumptions. Firstly, they have pointed to the fact that language codifies a particular worldview; it gives a name and a particular definition to what might otherwise be seen as neutral acts. For example, those terms related to sex and sexuality often encode a male perspective. Cameron (1985) discusses terms such as *penetration, fuck, screw, lay,* all of which turn heterosexual sex into something that men do to women. *Penetration,* from a female perspective, could be given more appropriate names such as *enclosure, surrounding, engulfing.* In a similar way, the absense of names representing women's perceptions and experiences also reveals a male bias. Gloria Steinem sees terms such as *sexual harassment* and *sexism* as significant in this respect: "A few years ago, they were just called life" (Steinem 1983, 149).

Secondly, feminist theorists have invoked linguistic determinism and the Sapir–Whorf hypothesis (Whorf 1956) to justify the need for language reform. If language is not a neutral vehicle in the representation of reality, then the potential influence of language on attitudes and perceptions is crucial. Indeed, linguistic determinism is the idea that the structure of one's language determines one's perceptions.

According to the Sapir–Whorf hypothesis, the grammatical distinctions and categories of one's native language determine the way one thinks about and/or perceives the world. For example, Hopi (an Amerindian language investigated by Whorf) distinguishes grammatically between the hypothetical as opposed to the non-hypothetical nature of an event but not between events occurring in the present or past. Therefore, Hopi-speakers are said to have a different conception of time than do English-speakers since English does grammaticize tense. According to Whorf, differences in the way that various cultural groups think about the world are thought to be a direct function of the grammatical and lexical properties of a group's language.

The significance of the Sapir–Whorf hypothesis for language reform is clear: if language has the powerful influence over thoughts and perceptions that Whorf suggests, then language reform is an essential part of the eradication of sexual inequalities. On the other hand, if speakers are not bound, conceptually or perceptually, by the limits of their language, then language reform would seem less essential to the goal of social change.

Although the Sapir–Whorf hypothesis is an appealing one, it does not have many subscribers, at least in the strong form presented above. There are several problems. Firstly, even if a language does not make a particular grammatical or lexical distinction, it does not follow that its speakers will be unable to conceptualize that distinction. David Crystal (1987) cites some Australian aboriginal languages that have very few words for numbers: there may be a few general words such as *all, many, few,* and then words for *one* and *two.* This, of course, does not mean that speakers of such languages will be unable to count or perform numerical computations.

Further, Sapir and Whorf tended to overestimate the differences among the languages of the world. All languages share many grammatical and lexical properties. This emphasis on language universals has made it difficult to attribute the different perceptions of cultural groups to differences in language.

Nonetheless, a weaker version of the Sapir–Whorf hypothesis is generally accepted. The comments of Frank (1989) and Cameron (1990) are typical.

> Few would suggest that sexual or racial inequality exists because of language use. Nor would many argue that banishing sexist and racist labeling would in itself result in a just society. At the same time, it is clear that language not only reflects social structures but, more important, sometimes serves to perpetuate existing differences in power; thus a serious concern with linguistic usage is fully warranted. (Frank 1989, 109)

> Like other representations (for example, those of the visual arts), linguistic representations both give a clue to the place of women

in the culture and constitute one means whereby we are kept in our place. (Cameron 1990, 12)

Even a weak version of the Sapir–Whorf hypothesis, however, is incompatible with the "language-as-symptom" view, which posits that language has no power to influence behaviour, perceptions, or attitudes. In this view, language simply mirrors changes in perceptions and attitudes. Language is seen as independent of the social world, as separate, autonomous, and only occasionally influenced by social factors.

By contrast, many have argued that language is a social phenomenon:

> Linguistic phenomena are social in the sense that whenever people speak or listen or write or read, they do so in ways which are determined socially and have social effects. Even when people are most conscious of their own individuality, and think themselves to be most cut off from social influences—"in the bosom of the family," for example—they still use language in ways which are subject to social convention. And the ways in which people use language in the most intimate and private encounters are not only socially determined by the social relationships of the family, they also have social effects in the sense of helping to maintain (or, indeed, change) those relationships. (Fairclough 1989, 23)

Indeed, some research demonstrates that language reform is an integral part of social change.

Nan Van den Bergh (1987) discusses the way in which renaming has been linked to empowerment. In the 1960s, black activists adopted the term *black* as opposed to *coloured* or *Negro* as a symbol of black people's control over their own identity. Van den Bergh shows that this type of language reform is psychologically powerful in raising consciousness within oppressed groups as well as carrying a message to groups in power. Similarly, the "naming" of female perceptions and experiences can be a source of women's empowerment, which, in itself, is linked to social change.

Feminist discussions of language (i.e., language reform) have sensitized individuals to ways in which language is discriminatory towards women. Sally McConnell-Ginet (1989) points to the fact that it is getting harder and harder to make *he* function as a true generic because of the controversy around its so-called generic use. In other words, language has become one of the arenas in which social inequalities have been elucidated. Disputes and debates over language, rather than being merely an outgrowth of social realities, are in fact, an integral part of social change.

INSTITUTIONAL AND INDIVIDUAL CHANGE

We will go on to evaluate the progress that has been made during the last two decades in the area of communication reform. But first we should distinguish between institutional and individual change. By institutional change, we mean changes made in agencies, companies, and organizations in the form of policy statements and/or guidelines. By individual change, we mean change in a person's private life as well as change that occurs within an institution but that is left to the discretion of an individual.

Institutional change █

In Canada, nonsexist language is widely regarded as an essential component in achieving employment equity in the workplace. As a result, a number of universities, businesses, and other organizations have included such policies in their employment equity programs and have adopted language guidelines.

Language also plays a part in general anti-discrimination initiatives. For instance, a 1990 University of Alberta plan, intended to reduce discrimination against women on campus, calls for professors to eliminate sexist language from their educational materials.✦ Some universities have addressed the issue of spoken as well as written language by including questions on language usage in teaching evaluations.✦✦ A number of professional organizations, including the Canadian Association of University Teachers, no longer publish job advertisements using *he/man* language. As of July 1988, the CAUT Bulletin no longer accepts ads with gender-exclusive language "except when that language has been mandated by human rights legislation [i.e., affirmative action measures]."

Municipal, provincial, and federal governments in Canada have made changes, as have their U.S. counterparts. For example, *Canada Manpower* has become *Employment and Immigration Canada*. In 1990, Toronto Metro councillors voted by a 12–7 margin to recommend that the federal government make changes in the wording of the national anthem. (They recommend replacing "true patriot love in all thy *sons* command" with "true patriot love in all of *us* command.") Organizations as diverse as Ontario Hydro, the United Church of Canada, and Canadian National now have nonsexist guidelines.

The issue of inclusive language has been an important (and controversial) one for several Christian denominations, including the United Church of Canada and the Anglican Church of Canada, both of which have produced nonsexist language guidelines. In 1989, the pastoral team of the Canadian Conference of Catholic Bishops advocated a move from exclusive to inclusive language in official texts and also in the everyday language of the church.◇ In more liberal Christian denominations there seems to be acceptance of nonsexist language in addressing and referring to clergy and church members but somewhat more resistance in the area of altering Biblical texts. Nonsexist reference to God (e.g., as *the parent* instead of as *the father*) is often seen as problematic. A contributer to a 1991 issue of the *Presbyterian Record* writes that "so-called 'sexist' language for God doesn't bother [him] because to [him] the nouns and pronouns used to refer to God are figures of speech without any sexual connotations."◇◇

While Orthodox Judaism has not changed, some North American reform, conservative, and reconstructionist movements have fought for the use of in-

---

✦ *Globe and Mail*, 24 Aug. 1990.

✦✦ This has been implemented at the University of Toronto Law School and is under consideration for Osgoode Hall Law School (York University).

◇ "Bishops Urge Equality in Revised Church Texts," *Toronto Star*, 19 Aug. 1989.

◇◇ Burdett McNeel, "Inclusive Language," *Presbyterian Record*, Feb. 1991, 35.

clusive language both in Hebrew and in English. Great progress has been made in modifying the English of the liturgy in progressive Jewish groups, but to date there is little evidence that the same is happening in the Hebrew liturgy. This may be partially explained by the fact that most North Americans do not know Hebrew well and thus are not as offended by sexist references in that language. Also, language reform in Hebrew is a complex task since Hebrew makes even greater use of grammatical gender than does French. Efforts to make Hebrew more inclusive include frequent use of *sheshina* "one who protects," a synonym for God that is feminine in gender.❖

Compliance with institutional change is not always uniform, particularly when it is seen as conflicting with other principles and policies. For example, while sexist course titles such as "*Man* and *His* Environment" have virtually disappeared, some individuals and departments still appeal to their academic freedom to name courses as they wish. Likewise, in an institution with formally adopted nonsexist guidelines, individuals may still contend that they are free to write as they choose (often citing the objections to reform we outlined in chapter 1).

In some cases, institutional change proceeds only slowly. Several staple stylebooks now include sections on nonsexist language, emphasizing the need to avoid sexual stereotyping. But the *Canadian Press Style Book* (1984, 237) goes on to call it "proper English" to use *he* to refer to both genders. And while it admits that "some" reject *man* for excluding women and suggest writing *people* or *human beings* instead, it warns, "But don't go overboard. To write *human energy* or *human resources* simply to avoid *manpower*, or *person-eating* tiger to avoid *man-eating tiger* is to suggest hypersensitivity" (p. 238).

The 1990 *Globe and Mail Style Book* is better. It recognizes the problem with the "generic" *he* and suggests pluralization or recasting the sentence. However, "*he or she*" and "*his or her*" are to be used only as "a last resort" and use of *s/he* and *he–she* is prohibited. Likewise, while it suggests that the use of *man* to include both sexes is to be avoided (e.g., *policeman* ➤ *police officer*), it advocates gender-specific "solutions" such as *spokesman/spokeswoman, chairman/chairwoman,* etc.

In a longitudinal study of a number of U.S. newspapers, Ralph Fasold (1988) found that a newspaper's (non)sexist language policy correlated positively with (non)sexist language use in the newspaper. For example, he reports that "changes in language-use policy over the years have succeeded in practically eliminating the discriminatory practice of referring to married women by their husbands' names only" (p. 202). While newspapers aimed at a general readership do not take the lead in bringing about change, "if the new practices and the motivations that prompt them become sufficiently widespread in the general society, the printed news media may then introduce new policies and they will be carried out explicitly" (p. 202). News agencies' capacity to enforce policy is of course crucial. In this regard, Fasold (pp. 205–06) mentions an article appearing in the *Washington Post*, which gave a clear insight into that newspaper's enforcement of its policy: "The reporter had just referred to a woman by last name alone in a second reference, when he added parenthetically: 'This newspaper's rules require that I call her merely that, though I would prefer Mrs.———.'"

❖ Personal communication, David Mendelsohn.

Individual change ▮

While individual change is harder to document than institutional change, it is clear that awareness of the issue is much greater than it was a decade ago. A 1990 study by Suzanne Levesque, which replicated the Briere and Lanktree study of the effect of the "generic" *he* on career choice, found a high degree of awareness of the language issue amongst undergraduate students. After the main task of the study was completed, Levesque solicited respondents' written comments. Student remarks included:

> The persistent use of "he, man, his" . . . is offensive. In the quote "man's understanding of himself and others"—are the women others? If so, then women are put in the same category as animals.

> A career in psychology for women is not that attractive from the above paragraph because throughout the paragraph there is only man, himself, he and his mentioned. There is no mentioning [*sic*] of women, herself or she. It seems that psychology is a very patriarchal profession, so therefore it would make a woman feel unaccepted and left out if she joined such a career.

However, a 1988 study by Hillary Allen found that undergraduates, and women in particular, repeatedly chose *he* when required to complete sentences containing neutral terms such as *jogger* ("When the jogger finished the 5 km run, ———"). Yet in another component of the study, the women interpreted *he* as exclusionary and expressed a strong desire for language reform. Clearly, there can still be a gap between attitudes and actual behaviour.

Another problem concerns the misunderstanding and/or misuse of nonsexist terms. Because linguistic meanings are, to a great extent, socially constructed and constituted (i.e., the way people use words is not based solely on dictionary meanings), nonsexist terms may be appropriated by a sexist speech community and/or culture. In chapter 7 we saw that the term *Ms*, intended to be a neutral title to parallel *Mr.*, is used by some as a title for divorced women and by others as a replacement for *Miss*. The predominant values and attitudes of a culture (in this case, a culture's preoccupation with a woman's relationship to a man) may in the end determine how nonsexist terms get used. Thus, while institutions may legislate language reform in their policies, the extent to which individuals or speech communities adopt nonsexist usage will vary.

CHANGE   IN   FRENCH: ▮
CANADA   AND   FRANCE ▮

We mentioned in chapter 5 that language reform in Quebec and in France has taken different paths.✤ The following story will serve to illustrate this. Recently, a colleague worked with the program committee for a conference at a major university in France. As she had expected, she found the French to be more

---

✤ For an overview of recent French feminist thought see Toril Moi (1985, 1987) and, for the 1970s and earlier, the works of Gisèle Halimi and Simone de Beauvoir.

conservative than French-speakers elsewhere (nonsexist alternatives were accepted only if there was a readily available feminine version such as *président/présidente*). But she was startled by the hostility towards feminizing any French word not part of that tradition. Well-known French feminists objected to *professeure* and *rapporteure* or *rapporteuse*. In contrast, some Canadian scholars would not participate unless they were listed as *professeures*. This problem was solved by omitting all titles from the program.

Comparison of Canadian and French women's magazines reveals the same tendencies. In the article "Les Femmes de Pouvoir" in the French magazine *Marie-Claire* (Sept. 1989), the majority of references to France's powerful women contained masculine job titles such as *deputé* au Parlement européen, *chef* des affaires monétaires, *président* du tribunal, and *ingénieur* d'armements aux arsenaux. Although the francophone edition of the Canadian magazine *Châtelaine* contains many more feminine job titles, usage is still somewhat inconsistent. Not all titles are feminized, and in some cases, as we saw in chapter 5, there is still no consensus as to which alternatives to use.

CHANGE AND VISUAL IMAGES

Even among those institutions that have adopted nonsexist language policies, few have tackled the problem of sexism in visual images. At York University, for example, although a policy on gender-biased language is in place, the university is officially silent about gender-biased images, and no help is available in the university's 1985 style guide.

There are exceptions. Advertising councils in Canada and elsewhere have guidelines relating to biased depictions of women. But these guidelines are voluntary and do not seem to have had much effect. Much advertising is still gender-biased.◆

The publishing house McGraw-Hill (one of the first to issue language guidelines) has a policy regarding images, and the University of Toronto covers visual material as well as language in its 1989 "Gender Neutral Guidelines" produced by the Status of Women office. The University of Toronto recommends that in photographs and illustrations, women and men should be depicted:

> with relatively equal frequency; at all levels of authority and participation; in reasonable numbers in nontraditional or unstereotypical roles, occupations or activities; representing varied ages, races, ethnic groups and human characteristics; with clothing, posture, expression and gesture conveying equal status and respect. (University of Toronto *Bulletin*, 30 Oct. 1989)

◆ In 1990, one of Canada's major breweries ran an advertisement depicting a woman as a "fox." The Toronto Transit Commission refused to allow the ad to be placed on its property. The offending advertisement was finally withdrawn, though the brewery continued to claim that it was not gender-biased and that it in fact depicted women in a positive light! At the same time, Canada's other major brewery was running an advertisement focussing on a woman referred to as "La Goddess." Marketing reporter Marina Strauss gives a good analysis of the controversy surrounding these two advertisements in the *Globe and Mail*, 20 July 1990.

Lack of institutional change has led to individuals and groups taking their own action. Billboards featuring gender-biased posters are often defaced; posters are removed from public walls; interest groups, such as the Vancouver-based Media Watch, are formed to monitor media content as it relates to women.

GUIDELINES FOR PROMOTING INSTITUTIONAL CHANGE

Roberta Hall and Bernice Sandler's highly influential 1982 "Chilly Climate" report on the negative environment experienced by women at university contains an extensive set of guidelines for increasing awareness and facilitating change in the university setting. Here we adapt some of their suggestions to deal specifically with nonsexist language and visual images in colleges and universities, businesses, government offices, and other organizations.

Administrators and executive officers

- Issue a policy statement against sexual stereotyping, sexist language, and sexist visual images. Ensure that members of the organization are aware of the institutional commitment by: distributing the policy statement to current employees (and, in the case of universities or colleges, students); making it part of the package of materials distributed to new employees (and students); and publishing the policy statement in internal bulletins or newsletters.
- Include the nonsexist communication policy in the organization's mission statement or academic plan.
- Introduce guidelines for use of nonsexist language and images (either taken from outside sources or developed specifically for the institution). Accompany this with workshops that present the rationale for such guidelines and provide instruction for implementation.
- In the case of colleges and universities, include in student evaluations questions such as: Does this teacher treat women's and men's comments with the same degree of seriousness? Use sexist humour? Use gender-balanced classroom examples?

Instructors in colleges, universities, and schools

- Become aware of your classroom behaviour (by tape recording your class, by having a colleague observe your class, by reviewing student questionnaires) to determine whether or not you treat or refer to female and male students differently. For example, do you treat female and male students' comments with the same degree of seriousness? Do you use sexist humour?
- Use parallel terminology in addressing male and female students and avoid reference to female students' appearance, unless you make similar reference to male students.
- Evaluate texts (and other teaching materials) critically. Where possible, avoid those that use sexual stereotyping and sexist language or images.

Company and government employees

- Become aware of your behaviour in meetings, presentations, and interactions with co-workers and clients to determine whether or not you treat women and

men differently. For example, do you treat women's and men's comments with the same degree of seriousness? Do you use sexist humour?
• Use parallel terminology in addressing and referring to male and female clients and co-workers and avoid reference to women's appearance, home lives, and so on, unless you make similar reference to males.
• Evaluate company materials critically. Avoid sexual stereotyping and sexist language or images.

Students

• Familiarize yourself with your institution's sexual harassment policy. Sexist humour and sexual stereotyping create a negative environment for work and study and can be interpreted as sexual harassment.
• Use your student evaluation form to comment (positively and negatively) on your classes.
• Encourage student publications to write about these issues.
• Where appropriate, discuss problems of classroom climate with the department's chair or sexual harassment centre staff.

CONCLUSION

The implementation of a nonsexist communication policy does not guarantee immediate and total compliance. However, nonsexist communication policies sanction the initiatives of proponents of reform. They can also be persuasive for individuals who might not agree with, or feel strongly about, language reform but who see themselves as team players or company people. Most importantly, such policies highlight the way in which language reflects and contributes to social inequalities. And it is only through raising awareness of these inequalities that social change can be effected.

FURTHER READING

Francine Frank and Paula Treichler, *Language, Gender, and Professional Writing* (New York: Modern Language Association, 1989).
♦ See articles by Francine Frank, Sally McConnell-Ginet, and Paula Treichler for further discussion of the relationship between language reform and social change.

Roberta Hall and Bernice Sandler, "The Classroom Climate: A Chilly One for Women?"
♦ A 1982 report available from the Project on the Status and Education of Women, Association of American Colleges, 1818 R St. NW, Washington DC, USA 20009. Parts are reprinted in Appendix 1 of Whithers' article "Resources for Liberating the Curriculum" in Joyce Penfield, ed., *Women and Language in Transition* (Albany: State University of New York Press, 1987).

English Terms

This appendix is organized as follows. Sexist terms are presented in alphabetical order with appropriate nonsexist alternatives. For example, to find a substitute for *chairman*, look up *chairman* and you will find *chair* listed as a nonsexist alternative. The appendix consists largely of terms discussed in the preceding chapters. For more extensive nonsexist glossaries/dictionaries, see Rosalie Maggio's *The Nonsexist Word Finder* and Cheris Kramarae and Paula Treichler's *A Feminist Dictionary*.

actress > actor

alderman > councillor

alumni *(Latin masculine plural form)* > graduates, former students

alumnus *(Latin masculine singular form)* > graduate, former student

anchorman > anchor, newscaster

authoress > author

baby > *use only to refer to infants of either sex*

bachelor/bachelorette > single person *(use if marital status is to be specified)*

ballerina > ballet dancer

barmaid > bartender

barman > bartender

benefactress > benefactor

boyfriend > friend, partner, date, person you are seeing, companion, lover, significant other

brothers *(generic)* > brothers and sisters, colleagues

businessman > business person, business executive

business woman > business person, business executive

cameraman > camera operator

chairman/chairwoman > chair, chairperson

chambermaid > housekeeper, room cleaner, room attendant

choirmaster > choir director

cleaning lady > cleaner

clergyman > clergy, member of the clergy, cleric, priest

coed > student

comedienne > comedian

councilman > councillor

countryman > citizen

craftsman > craftsperson, artisan

craftsmanship > craftwork, artisanship

don > tutor, professor

draftsman > draftsperson

every man for himself > everyone for themselves

faculty wife > faculty spouse *(use only if marital status is to be specified)*

fellow *(adjective)* > associated, related

fellow *(noun)* > friend, colleague, acquaintance, associate *(of a college)*

female doctor, female dentist, female garbage collector, > doctor, dentist, garbage collector

fireman > firefighter

forefathers > ancestors

fraternal > warm, intimate

fraternity > companionship, unity, association

freshman > first-year student

garbageman > garbage collector

gentlemen's agreement > verbal agreement, informal contract

girl > *use only to refer to female children; use* woman *to refer to adult females (see chapter 4)*

girlfriend > friend, partner, date, person you are seeing, companion, lover, significant other

grantsmanship > grant-getting ability

groundsman > groundskeeper

handyman > handyperson

he/him/his/himself > *use only to refer to a male; use true generics such as singular* they, s/he, he or she, she or he, she/he, *etc. (see chapter 3)*

heiress > heir

heroine > hero, heroic figure, protagonist

hostess > host

housemaid > household worker, cleaner

lady > woman

lady dentist, lady doctor, lady garbage collector > dentist, doctor, garbage collector

landlady > building owner, proprietor

landlord > building owner, proprietor

layman > layperson

maid > household worker, cleaner

maiden name > birth name, surname

mailman > letter carrier

majorette > baton twirler, marching band leader

man/men > *use only to refer to males; use true generics such as* people, humans, humanity, *etc. (see chapter 2)* man *(verb)* > staff, run, work, operate

man and wife > husband and wife

man in the street > the average person

manageress > manager

manful > brave

manhole > access hole

manhole cover > sewer cover

manhood > adulthood

mankind > humanity

manly > courageous, direct

man-made > manufactured, synthetic

manpower > human resources, staff, personnel (Canada Manpower *is now* Employment and Immigration Canada)

manslaughter > *has a specific legal meaning and is an offence under the Criminal Code; in general contexts, you can use* killing *or* murder

master *(adjective)* > expert, acomplished

master *(noun)* > head, principal, director *(e.g. of a college)*, owner, president

master *(verb)* > learn, become an expert in, acquire proficiency in

meter maid > meter attendant

middleman > go-between

Miss > *use* Ms *unless you know that the particular individual prefers* Miss *(see chapter 7)*

Mrs. > *use* Ms *unless you know that the particular individual prefers* Mrs. *(see chapter 7)*

newsman > newscaster, reporter

night watchman > night guard, night watch

office girl > office assistant, secretary

ombudsman > ombudsperson, ombuds officer

patroness > patron

penmanship > handwriting

poetess > poet

policeman > police officer, police constable

policewoman > police officer, police constable

proprietress > proprietor

repairman > repairer *(or more specifically,* plumber, electrician, *etc.)*

salesgirl > salesperson, sales clerk

saleslady > salesperson, sales clerk

salesman > salesperson, sales clerk

saleswoman > salesperson, sales clerk

sculptress > sculptor

seductress > seducer

self-made man > self-made person, entrepreneur

showman > performer

songstress > singer

sons *(generic)* > children, daughters and sons, sons and daughters

spinster > single person *(use when marital status is to be specified)*

spokesman > spokesperson

sportsman > athlete, sports lover, hunter

sportsmanlike > fair, sporting

statesman > government leader, politician, public servant

statesmanlike > stately, distinguished, diplomatic

stewardess > flight attendant

straw man > irrelevant argument, red herring

waitress > waiter, server

weatherman > weather forecaster

woman dentist, woman doctor, woman garbage collector > dentist, doctor, garbage collector

working mother > wage-earner (working mother *implies that un-*

paid work done in the home is not work)

workman > worker

workman's compensation > worker's compensation

workmanship > craftwork, work, artisanship

Some Problems

Sometimes there is no simple nonsexist alternative to a term in widespread usage. Paraphrasing is one way round the difficulty, as is rethinking the sentence.

For example, *housewife* is sometimes rendered "member of the unpaid labour force." This is both unclear and cumbersome. Indeed, the concept *housewife* is open to question: does it apply to the person who cleans the house regardless of whether s/he has a paid job elsewhere? Regardless of whether that person is male or female? Does the alternative *househusband* sound merely ludicrous? Does looking for a nonsexist alternative mask the fact that women, whether or not they spend eight hours a day in the paid labour force, still carry primary responsibility for looking after houses, children, older family members, and, of course, the men they live with?

Householder and *homeowner* are not exact equivalents as many housewives do not own the homes they clean and caretake. Many women who stay home to look after their families prefer the term *homemaker*. We need to be quite clear what we are specifying.

> *Housewives* can buy more cheaply at their local market.
> ➤ *Shoppers* can buy more cheaply at their local market.

> *Housewives* can keep their homes cleaner with Brand X.
> ➤ *Homes* can be kept cleaner with Brand X.

In some cases, no consensus has been reached as as to whether the term in question is sexist or not. Degree titles furnish some good examples. Certainly the effect of Bachelor of Arts, Master of Arts on the ear is unfortunate (see chapter 2 on *man*), yet it is often maintained that the *bachelor* in *Bachelor* of Science is now unrelated to that in *bachelor*, "an unmarried male." If degree titles are to be changed, we recommend non-specific alternatives such as *baccalaureate*. In the case of *masters*, we do not know of a good gender-neutral term (*first graduate degree* is too general). The use of initials, as in MA, BSc, is widely understood. We look forward to the debate on the subject and the emergence of gender-neutral alternatives.

French Terms

This appendix is organized alphabetically. Most entries contain a masculine and a feminine form. For example, to find the feminine equivalent of *agent*, look up *agent* and you will find *agente*. If only one form appears, use *une* or *la* to make it feminine, e.g. *une témoin* and *une biologiste*. In certain cases we have included more than one possible feminine equivalent. The form we advocate is listed first.

Recent editions of standard French dictionaries have begun to include feminine forms for job titles previously only used in the masculine. The following list consists largely of feminine terms not yet found in traditional dictionaries.

agriculteur > agricultrice

agronome

amateur > amatrice

annonceur > annnonceure

annonceur-présentateur > annon-
ceure-présentatrice

anthropologue

apiculteur > apicultrice

appariteur > apparitrice

architecte

armurier > armurière

arrangeur > arrangeuse

assureur > assureuse

auteur > auteure

avocat > avocate

banquier > banquière

biologiste

cadre

cadreur > cadreuse

camionneur > camioneuse

capitaine

cartographe

chancelier > chancelière

chargé > chargée

chargé de cours > chargée de cours

chargé de mission > chargée de
  mission

charpentier > charpentière

chauffeur > chauffeuse

chef

chercheur > chercheuse

commis-vendeur > commis-ven-
  deuse

commissaire

compositeur > compositrice

conférencier > conférencière

conseil

conseiller > conseillère

conservateur > conservatrice

consul > consule

consultant > consultante

contractuel > contractuelle

contrôleur > contrôleuse

critique

cytologiste

débardeur > débardeuse

défenseur > défenseuse

demandeur > demandeuse

dépanneur > dépanneuse

député > députée

détacheur > détacheuse

diplomate

directeur > directrice

docteur > docteure

doyen > doyenne

ébéniste

éclairagiste

économiste-conseil

écrivain > écrivaine

électricien > électricienne

émissaire

estimateur > estimatrice

évaluateur > évaluatrice

expert > experte

financier > financière

géologue

gestionnaire

gouverneur > gouverneure

graphiste

graveur > graveuse

greffier > greffière

guetteur > guetteuse

historien > historienne

homme d'affaires > femme
  d'affaires

horticulteur > horticultrice

illustrateur > illustratrice

installateur > installatrice

infirmier > infirmière

ingénieur > ingénieure

instituteur > institutrice

instructeur > instructrice

interne

juge

lieutenant-gouverneur > lieutenante-gouverneure

machiniste

magasinier > magasinière

maire > maire, mairesse

maître > maître, maîtresse *(in certain usages only; see chapter 5)*

maître-assistant > maître-assistante

mannequin

manoeuvre

marin

matelot

mécanicien > mécanicienne

médecin

membre

menuisier > menuisière

mesureur > mesureuse

métallurgiste

metteur en scène > metteure en scène

mineur > mineuse

ministre > ministre, ministresse

mouliste

notaire > notaire, notairesse

officier > officière

opérateur > opératrice

orateur > oratrice

outilleur > outilleuse

peintre

physiothérapeute

pilote

pisciculteur > piscicultrice

plombier > plombière

podiâtre

poète

policier > policière

pompier > pompière

président > présidente

professeur > professeure, professeuse, professoresse

professionnel > professionnelle

programmeur > programmeuse

rapporteur > rapporteuse

recruteur > recruteuse

recteur > rectrice

régisseur > régisseuse

registraire

reporteur > reporteuse

savant > savante

sculpteur > sculpteure

sénateur > sénatrice

serrurier > serrurière

soigneur > soigneuse

sous-chef

sous-directeur > sous-directrice

substitut

superviseur > superviseure

tailleur > tailleuse

tarificateur > tarificatrice

technologue

témoin

tôlier > tôlière

trempeur > trempeuse

trompette

usager > usagère

vendeur > vendeuse

zoologiste

Terms of address in French

- *Mad.* — use as the parallel title abbreviation to *M*.
- *Madame* — use for adult females, regardless of marital status (see chapter 7). In writing, the usual abbreviation is *Mme*. However, we advocate the use of *Mad.*, the abbreviation for *Madelle*, in written discourse.
- *Madelle* — use for adult females, regardless of marital status (not widely used, however: see chapter 7). In writing, the abbreviation is *Mad*.
- *Mademoiselle* — avoid for adult females, unless you know it is the personal preference of the particular woman.

Reference List

Adbusters Quarterly. Vancouver: Adbusters Media Foundation.

Allen, Hillary. 1988. "Generic Pronoun Choice as a Measure of 'Concrete' Behavioural Intent." *Journal of the Atlantic Provinces Linguistic Association* 10: 111–39.

Arnold, Edmond C. 1969. *Modern Newspaper Design*. New York: Harper and Row.

Atkinson, Donna. 1987. "Names and Titles: Maiden Name Retention and the Use of Ms." *Journal of the Atlantic Provinces Linguistic Association* 9: 56–84.

Barnes, Judith A. 1984. "Gender Portrayal in Magazine Advertising: A Comparative Analysis of Three Elements of Gender Imagery in Magazine Ads in 1953, 1979, and 1983: Faces, Places, and Products." PhD diss., Rensselaer Polytechnic Institute, Troy, NY.

Baron, Dennis. 1986. *Grammar and Gender*. New Haven: Yale University Press.

Barrett, Neil Jr. 1990. "Winter on the Belle Fourche." In *The Year's Best Science Fiction*, ed. Gardner Dozois. New York: St. Martin's Press.

Bem, Sandra, and Darryl Bem. 1973. "Does Sex-Biased Advertising 'Aid and Abet' Sex Discrimination?" *Journal of Applied Social Psychology* 3: 6–18.

Benveniste, Emile. 1966. *Problèmes de linguistique générale*. Paris: Gallimard.

Berger, John, Sven Blomberg, Chris Fox, Michael Dibb, and Richard Hollis, eds. 1972. *Ways of Seeing*. London: Penguin Books.

Bodine, Ann. 1975. "Androcentrism in Prescriptive Grammar." *Language in Society* 4, 2: 129–46.

Boel, Else. 1976. "Le genre des noms désignant les professions et les situations féminines en français moderne." *Revue Romane* 11, 1: 16–73.

Bogart, Leo. 1967. *Strategies in Advertising*. New York: Harcourt, Brace and World.

Briere, John, and Cheryl Lanktree. 1983. "Sex Role Related Effects of Sex Bias in Language." *Sex Roles* 9: 625–32.

Brown, Roger, and Albert Gilman. 1960. "The Pronouns of Power and Solidarity." In *Style in Language*, ed. Thomas A. Sebeok. Cambridge, MA: MIT Press.

Butler, Matilda, and William Paisley. 1980. *Women and the Mass Media*. New York: Human Sciences Press.

Cameron, Deborah. 1985. *Feminism and Linguistic Theory*. London: Macmillan.

Cameron, Deborah, ed. 1980. *The Feminist Critique of Language*. London: Routledge.

Clarke, Sandra. 1989. "Language and Sex: A Bibliography." *Women and Language* 12, 2: 9–20.

Coates, Jennifer. 1986. *Women, Men and Language*. New York: Longman.

Communicating Without Bias. 1990. Toronto: Ontario Hydro.

Council of Ontario Universities. 1988. *Employment Equity for Women: A University Handbook*. Toronto.

Courtney, Alice E., and Thomas W. Whipple. 1983. *Sex Stereotyping in Advertising*. Lexington, MA: Lexington Books.

Crawford, Mary, and Linda English. 1984. "Generic Versus Specific Inclusions of Women in Language: Effects on Recall." *Journal of Psycholinguistic Research* 13: 373–81.

Creative Source. 1990. Toronto: Wilcord Publications.

Crystal, David. 1987. *The Cambridge Encyclopedia of Language*. Cambridge: Cambridge University Press.

Daiches, David. 1970. "The Nature of Virginia Woolf's Art." In *Critics on Virginia Woolf*, ed. Jacqueline Latham. London: George Allen and Unwin.

Daly, Mary. 1978. *Gyn/ecology: The Metaethics of Radical Feminism*. Toronto: Fitzhenry & Whiteside.

Daly, Mary, and Jane Caputi. 1987. *Websters' First New Intergalactic Wickedary of the English Language*. Boston: Beacon Press.

Dayhoff, Signe. 1983. "Sexist Language and Person Perception: Evaluation of Candidates from Newspaper Articles." *Sex Roles* 9: 527–38.

Dumais, Hélène. 1987. *La féminisation des titres et du discours au Québec: Une bibliographie*. Les Cahiers de recherche du GREMF (Groupe de recherche multidisciplinaire féministe). Quebec: Université Laval.

Dyer, Gillian. 1988. *Advertising as Communication*. London: Routledge.

Eakins, Barbara, and R. Gene Eakins. 1978. *Sex Differences in Human Communication*. Boston: Houghton Mifflin.

Eichler, Margrit. 1988. *Nonsexist Research Methods: A Practical Guide*. Boston: Allen and Unwin.

Eichler, Margrit, and Jeanne Lapointe. 1985. *On the Treatment of the Sexes in Research*. Ottawa: Social Science and Humanities Research Council of Canada.

Elgin, Suzette Haden. 1984. *Native Tongue*. New York: Day Books.

Fairclough, Norman. 1989. *Language and Power*. New York: Longman.

Fasold, Ralph. 1988. "Language Policy and Change: Sexist Language in the Periodical News Media." In *Language Spread and Language Policy*, ed. Peter H. Lowenberg. Washington: Georgetown University Press.

Fédération canadienne des enseignantes et des enseignants. 1985. *Le langage non sexiste: guide de rédaction*. Ottawa.

Fédération canadienne des enseignantes et des enseignants. 1990. *Pour le traitement égalitaire des femmes et des hommes dans les communications écrites—guide de rédaction*. Ottawa.

Fishman, Pamela. 1983. "Interaction: The Work Women Do." In *Language, Gender and Society*, ed. Barrie Thorne, Cheris Kramarae, and Nancy Henley. Rowley, MA: Newburg House.

Frank, Francine Wattman. 1989. "Language Planning, Language Reform, and Language Change: A Review of Guidelines for Nonsexist Usage." In *Language, Gender and Professional Writing*, ed. Francine Wattman Frank and Paula A. Treichler. New York: Modern Language Association.

Frank, Francine, and Frank Anshen. 1983. *Language and the Sexes*. Albany: State University of New York Press.

Frank, Francine Wattman, and Paula A. Treichler. 1989. *Language, Gender, and Professional Writing*. New York: Modern Language Association.

Franzwa, Helen. 1974. "Woman's Place in Semantic Space." Paper presented at the Speech Communication Association Convention, Chicago.

Fromkin, Victoria, and Robert Rodman. 1983. *An Introduction to Language*, 4th ed. New York: Holt, Rinehart and Winston.

Geis, Michael L. 1987. *The Language of Politics*. New York: Springer-Verlag.

Gilbert, Sandra, and Susan Gubar, eds. 1979. *Feminist Essays on Women Poets*. Bloomington: Indiana University Press.

Globe and Mail Style Guide. 1990. Toronto.

Goffman, Erving. 1987. *Gender Advertisements*. New York: Harper and Row.

Gombrich, E.H. 1972. "The Visual Image." In *Communication* (special issue of *Scientific American*). San Francisco: W.H. Freeman.

Graddol, David, and Joan Swann. 1989. *Gender Voices*. New York: Blackwell.

Grevisse, Maurice. 1988. *Le bon usage*. 9th ed. Gembloux, Belgium: Editions J. Duculot.

Guidelines for Bias-Free Publishing. n.d. Highstown, NJ: McGraw-Hill.

Guidelines for Inclusive Language. 1981. Toronto: United Church of Canada.

Hall, Roberta, and Bernice Sandler. 1982. "The Classroom Climate: A Chilly One for Women?" Washington: Project on the Status and Education of Women, Association of American Colleges.

Hoffman, Nancy Jo. 1972. "Sexism in Letters of Recommendation." *Modern Language Association Newsletter*. Sept.: 5–6.

Hofstadter, Douglas R. 1986. *Metamagical Themas*. Toronto: Bantam Books.

Kilbourne, Jean. 1979. *Killing Us Softly: Advertising Images of Women*. Cambridge, MA: Cambridge Documentary Films.

Kilbourne, Jean. 1987. *Still Killing Us Softly*. Cambridge, MA: Cambridge Documentary Films.

Kramarae, Cheris. 1981. *Women and Men Speaking*. Rowley, MA: Newbury House.

Kramarae, Cheris, and Paula A. Treichler. 1985. *A Feminist Dictionary*. Boston: Pandora Press.

Kramer, Cheris. 1975. "Sex-Linked Variations in Address Systems." *Anthropological Linguistics* 17: 198–210.

Lakoff, Robin. 1975. *Language and Woman's Place*. New York: Harper & Row.

Lapointe, Jeanne, et Margrit Eichler. 1985. *Le traitement objectif des sexes dans la recherche*. Ottawa: Conseil de recherches en sciences humaines du Canada.

Lee, Rhonda, ed. 1985. *Guide to Nonsexist Language and Visuals*. Madison, WI: University of Wisconsin.

Les uns et les unes: Guide de communication nonsexiste. 1988. Montreal: Canadien national. Available in English as *Striking a Balance: A Guide to Nonsexist Communication*.

Levesque, Suzanne. 1990. "On the Use of Generic He." Unpublished manuscript, York University.

Linguistic Inquiry. 1972–73. Vols. 3–4. Cambridge, MA: MIT Press.

MacKay, Donald G. 1983. "Prescriptive Grammar and the Pronoun Problem." In *Language, Gender and Society*, ed. Barrie Thorne, Cheris Kramarae, and Nancy Henley. Rowley, MA: Newbury House.

Maggio, Rosalie. 1988. *The Nonsexist Word Finder: A Dictionary of Gender-Free Usage*. Boston: Beacon Press.

Martyna, Wendy. 1978. "What Does 'He' Mean? Use of the Generic Masculine." *Journal of Communication* 28: 131–38.

Martyna, Wendy. 1983. "Beyond the he/man approach." In *Language, Gender and Society*, ed. Barrie Thorne, Cheris Kramarae, and Nancy Henley. Rowley, MA: Newbury House.

McConnell-Ginet, Sally. 1978. "Address Forms in Sexual Politics." In *Women's Language and Style*, ed. Douglas Butturff and E. Epstein. Akron OH: L and S Books.

McConnell-Ginet, Sally. 1989. "The Sexual (Re) Production of Meaning." In *Language, Gender and Professional Writing*, ed. Francine Frank and Paula Treichler. New York: Modern Language Association.

Miller, Casey, and Kate Swift. 1976. *Words and Women: New Language in New Times*. Garden City, NY: Doubleday.

Miller, Susan. 1975. "The Content of News Photos: Women's and Men's Roles." *Journalism Quarterly* 52, 1: 70–75.

Ministère de l'Education du Québec. 1988. *Pour un genre à part entière: Guide pour la rédaction de textes non sexistes*. Quebec.

Moi, Toril. 1985. *Sexual/Textual Politics: Feminist Literary Theory*. London: Methuen.

Moi, Toril. 1987. *French Feminist Thought: A Reader*. New York: Blackwell.

Moulton, Janice. 1981. "The Myth of the Neutral 'Man'." In *Sexist Language: A Modern Philosophical Analysis*, ed. Mary Vetterling-Braggin, Frederick A. Elliston, and Jane English. Towata, NJ: Littlefield, Adams.

Nelson, Roy Paul. 1983. *Publication Design*, 3rd ed. Dubusque, IA: Wm. C. Brown.

New Vision Technologies. 1990. *Presentation Task Force. Computer Clip Art*. Nepean, ON.

Office de la langue française du Québec. 1986. *Titres et fonctions au féminin: essai d'orientation de l'usage*. Quebec.

Pickens, Judy. 1985. *The Copy-to-Press Handbook*. New York: John Wiley & Sons.

Ransom, John Crowe. 1963. "Emily Dickinson: A Poet Restored." In *Emily Dickinson: A Collection of Critical Essays*. Ed. Richard B. Sewall. Englewood Cliffs, NJ: Prentice-Hall.

Reeves, Margaret. 1990. "Sexist Language Use in York University Publications." Unpublished manuscript, York University.

Rose, Jacqueline. 1986. "Jeffrey Masson and Alice James." *Oxford Literary Review* 8, 1–2: 185–92.

Sampson, Geoffrey. 1980. *Schools of Linguistics*. Stanford, CA: Stanford University Press.

Schulz, Muriel R. 1975. "The Semantic Derogation of Women." In *Language and Sex: Difference and Dominance*, ed. Barrie Thorne and Nancy Henley. Rowley, MA: Newbury House.

Spender, Dale. 1985. *Man Made Language*, 2nd ed. Boston: Routledge and Kegan Paul.

Stannard, Una. 1977. *Mrs. Man*. San Francisco: Germainbooks.

Steinem, Gloria. 1983. *Outrageous Acts and Everyday Rebellions*. New York: Holt, Rinehart and Winston.

Sykes, Mary. 1985. "Discrimination in Discourse." In *Handbook of Discourse Analysis*, vol. 4, ed. Teun A. Van Dijk. New York: Academic Press.

Tannen, Charles J., ed. 1983. *A Handbook of Magazine Publishing*. New Canaan, CT: Folio Publishing.

Tannen, Deborah. 1990a. "What's in a First Name?" In Ronald Adler and Neil Towne, *Looking Out/Looking In: Interpersonal Communication*. Fort Worth: Holt, Rinehart and Winston.

Tannen, Deborah. 1990b. *You Just Don't Understand: Talk Between the Sexes*. New York: Morrow.

Thorne, Barrie, Cheris Kramarae, and Nancy Henley, eds. 1983. *Language, Gender and Society*. Rowley, MA: Newbury House.

Treichler, Paula. 1989. "From Discourse to Dictionary: How Sexist Meanings are Authorized." In *Language, Gender and Professional Writing*, ed. Francine Wattman Frank and Paula Treichler. New York: Modern Language Association.

Trescases, Pierre. 1983. "Propositions pour une compétence culturelle chez l'apprenant et l'enseignant." *French Review* 1: 48–54.

Trudgill, Peter. 1985. "Preface." In Philip Smith, *Language, the Sexes and Society*. Oxford: Basil Blackwell.

Tuchman, Gaye, Arlene Kaplan Daniels, and James Benet, eds. 1978. *Hearth and Home: Images of Women in the Mass Media*. New York: Oxford University Press.

Van den Bergh, Nan. 1987. "Renaming: Vehicle for Empowerment." In *Women and Language in Transition*, ed. Joyce Penfield. Albany: State University of New York Press.

Vetterling-Braggin, Mary, Frederick A. Elliston, and Jane English, eds. 1977. *Feminism and Philosophy*. Totawa, NJ: Littlefield, Adams.

Vignola, Marie-Josée. 1987. "Utilisation de titres professionnels masculins afin de désigner une femme: norme et usage." *York University Working Papers in Second-Language Teaching* 2: 55–82.

Vignola, Marie-Josée. 1990. "Quelques applications de la féminisation des titres en classe de français langue seconde." *Revue canadienne des langues vivantes* 46, 2: 354–64.

Watson, Carol. 1987. "Sex-Linked Difference in Letters of Recommendation." *Women and Language* 10, 2: 26–28.

Whitaker, Reginald. 1990. "Breaking the Mulroney Monopoly." *Canadian Forum* 118: 11–14.

Whithers, Barbara. 1987. "Resources for Liberating the Curriculum." In *Women and Language in Transition*, ed. Joyce Penfield. Albany: State University of New York Press.

Whorf, Benjamin. 1956. *Language, Thought and Reality: Selected Writings of Benjamin Lee Whorf.* Cambridge, MA: MIT Press.

Wolfson, Nessa, and Joan Manes. 1980. "Don't Dear Me!" In *Women and Language in Literature and Society*, ed. Sally McConnell-Ginet, Ruth Borker, and Nelly Furman. New York: Praeger.

Yaguello, Marina. 1978. *Les mots et les femmes.* Paris: Petite bibliothèque payot.

Yaguello, Marina. 1989. *Le sexe des mots.* Paris: Belfond.